Enhancing Learning through Play

Written to support early years professionals who are fascinated by the complexities and implications of early development, this fully updated second edition explains why children need to play and offers practical guidance on how best to support children's development and learning through play.

Based on a wealth of research in the field, this accessible and engaging book explores why children behave as they do at different ages and stages in their development and shows how play can complement and enhance their social, emotional, perceptual, motor and intellectual development. The author shows how detailed observations of children at play can lead to providing the most appropriate learning opportunities for children with different aptitudes and abilities.

Topics discussed include:

- the learning potential within different play activities;
- how emotional intelligence and children's self-esteem contribute to overall development;
- supporting children who find it difficult to play;
- gender bias;
- the nature versus nurture debate;
- using observations to ensure appropriate play experiences;
- ideas and strategies for carrying out small-scale research.

With suggestions for practitioner activities, and for action research questions that can be used for continuing professional development, this text is ideal for practitioners and students wanting to fully understand how play can enhance children's overall development.

Christine Macintyre, formerly a Fellow and Senior Lecturer at Moray House School of Education at the University of Edinburgh, is currently engaged in supporting the development of 'The Child's Journey' in Kirklees and providing guidelines for teachers of children with special needs in Kuwait. She does consultancy work at home and abroad on all aspects of children's development, particularly in the early years.

Enhancing Learning through Play

A developmental perspective
for early years settings

Second edition

Christine Macintyre

Routledge
Taylor & Francis Group

LONDON AND NEW YORK

First published 2001
by David Fulton Publishers

This second edition published 2012
by Routledge
2 Park Square, Milton Park, Abingdon, Oxon OX14 4RN

Simultaneously published in the USA and Canada
by Routledge
711 Third Avenue, New York, NY 10017

Routledge is an imprint of the Taylor & Francis Group, an informa business

British Library Cataloguing in Publication Data
A catalogue record for this book is available from the British Library

Library of Congress Cataloging-in-Publication Data
MacIntyre, Christine, 1938–
Enhancing learning through play : a developmental perspective for early
years settings / by Christine Macintyre. – 2nd ed.
p. cm.
Includes index.
1. Learning. 2. Play. 3. Creative ability in children. I. Title.
LB1060.M316 2012
372.21–dc22
2011012014

ISBN: 978-0-415-67124-8 (hbk)
ISBN: 978-0-415-67125-5 (pbk)
ISBN: 978-0-203-81446-8 (ebk)

Typeset in Bembo
by Keystroke, Station Road, Codsall, Wolverhampton

Printed and bound in Great Britain by
TJInternational Ltd, Padstow, Cornwall

Contents

Foreword

Practitioners working with young children have to contend with the pressures that come from parents and society about gaining the skills and abilities that are seen to be essential for school and later work. This can result in an over-formalisation of the type of opportunities that children may encounter in their earliest years. Added to this, there is the seductive nature of technology where the use of computers and other types of media is seen as crucial – even some 5-year-olds have mobile phones!

Amidst all this stands the child whose needs have not in fact changed over millennia – that is the need to feel loved, cared about, appreciated and also the need to find out about their world. This can only be done by experiencing the world within a context that is physically safe and developmentally appropriate. Christine's book powerfully reminds us that it is through play that all animals – including humans – learn. Children need to explore, to feel, taste, touch, hear, smell their world – in other words to encounter it fully so that they can, from the very beginning, find out the properties of all that is around them. Perhaps more than anything else, the shifts and style of play in which a child is engaged truly reflect how the child is developing from infancy onwards.

Play is, I believe, an essential part of early experience – it is the bridge between all aspects of development, emotional, social, physical and cognitive, and this book emphasises this crucial element. The opportunities for a young child to play by themselves or with a loved adult and later with other children and/or adults, together with the provision of other play resources, provide pieces of the jigsaw that supports the child's sense of self. This is achieved via the ongoing, parallel development in the child's growing understanding of both an emotional and physical self as experiences are accompanied by pleasure or frustration as skills and abilities are tried, tested and hopefully mastered. It is as if the properties of the self are being established as well as what constitutes the world outside.

For practitioners, therefore, an understanding of the importance of play is crucial. In her book, Christine notes that Vygotsky showed that the study of play and that of child development naturally complement each other. He claimed that, 'As in the focus of a magnifying glass, play contains all the developmental tendencies in a condensed form.' Watching children at play, it is possible to observe emotions, social interactions, physical development and the levels of the child's understanding and ability to make meaning from their experience. It is perhaps no wonder that in play, observers have often noted that the use of language is increased and that a child's self-confidence can emerge. It provides a window into the child's inner world, thereby helping us to understand their behaviour. In this way it is possible to see how play bridges emotions, learning and development.

The book itself has two main aims: the first is to support those who wish to understand the complexities of children's play, and the second is to provide study material for those who are seeking to gain new or further qualifications. Throughout there is an emphasis that in order to understand how and why children play and what they are learning from the different types of play, this requires *work* by the practitioners. Understanding is not simply observing – but what is *thought about* regarding those observations. Such thinking demands from the practitioner an understanding of the individual child set within a deep understanding of what supporting development actually means.

Each chapter begins with a brief résumé of the content, and the main format is the use of questions and answers. This provides a very useful forum as Christine has the ability to 'home in' on the type of questions that could be asked by practitioners when faced with what they are observing. The answers are indicative of her wealth of knowledge and experience as she not only provides potential answers but reflects on the issues which underpin those answers, thereby providing opportunities for further reflection and truly deep thinking about the child.

One of the most important issues for practitioners is the sensitivity required regarding when and how to intervene in children's play. This crucial topic is addressed in Chapter 2. One of the key factors addressed in Chapter 1 is that adults need to understand about play in the first instance and realise that it can take many forms and also be different between genders in its focus. It is so important as Christine points out that, 'in a play environment, the practitioners observe and begin from where the children are'.

Christine also provides a powerful rationale for practitioners and others involved with children to think about how sensory information, together with movement and the emotional context, provides children with an ongoing framework on which they build their understanding of themselves and others. Her detailed and clear explanations of the working of the senses can add to the armoury of practitioners and carers in understanding the needs and behaviour of a child. In particular, she highlights the difficulties children may encounter when they have over- or under-sensitivity to any specific sense as well as any problems with movement. Understanding that a child may be wary of being touched because of hypersensitivity to this sensation, borne out by careful observation of the child, would help practitioners to support the child in their day-to-day contact with other people as well as being alert to what stimuli the child may find difficult – e.g. feeling the cold keenly or disliking the feel of prickly objects.

This book provides practical advice which is underpinned by a wealth of knowledge regarding the fundamental aspects of feelings and relationships, the value of movement and the impact of sensory experience – in other words what is essential for a child to learn about themselves and their environment brought together by the types of play in which they wish to engage. Not all play is the same and different types of play emerge within different developmental time frames but what is crucial, as Christine points out, is that practitioners observe where the children actually are in their development and, importantly, where they are in each aspect of their development. This is because development does not occur in any of us in a straight line with every aspect at the same level. Observing children at play, however, provides a much more realistic picture of what the child can actually achieve and how they are able to manage their experiences. This allows practitioners to support a child to deal with the frustrations as well as the joys they might encounter during their play and thereby support their emotional well-being and behaviour.

This book is timely and important as it addresses the need for practitioners – and others – to understand the importance of play in the lives of children, that the opportunities to play, to interact, to experience vividly the world of the senses and movement are essential to helping children grow and learn. Technology is wonderful but perhaps not as wonderful, in the beautiful example given in this book, as throwing leaves into the air to paint the sky with rainbows.

Maria Robinson
May 2011

Introduction:
Let's Think about Play

This book is about observing children in different play environments and identifying what it is that they learn as they play. It is based around questions that parents, carers, friends and professionals ask as they reflect on the complexities of understanding development, learning, play and the interactions of all three and wonder how best to support each child. Current research and academic sources are considered in framing the answers. This is done to justify the responses and may be particularly important for those who wish to use this book as a basis for study. Throughout the text suggested activities are to stimulate reflection and discussion about the participation of different children as they learn and play.

From the outset, some children will enjoy playing and others will be more reluctant because play scenarios just like other learning experiences can be daunting. Sometimes children can tell us how they feel about their play; when this doesn't happen, parents and practitioners must listen as well as watch and record so that they can analyse all the learning that may be subtle and complex. The first activities consider the perspectives of two different children.

When I go to school each day,
I know there's time to play,
There's lots of toys and girls and boys,
What shall I do today?
I'd like to play with the big red truck,
If there isn't too much noise,
But usually, with my bad luck,
It's surrounded by big boys.
I can't bear messy things like clay,
And dressing up's no good.
What does it mean to wear strange clothes?
I wish I understood!
The bricks are best; I line them up,
Red, then white, then blue.
I love the patterns that they make,
It's the best thing that I do.

Activities

1. What you could glean about the play and learning ability of this 4-year-old?

2. What steps would you take to support him?

I really enjoy the water tray,
I make things sink and float.
At the sand I build a castle
Surrounded by a moat.
There are so many things to do
And we get to choose,
And so we win and know that we
Need never, ever, lose!

(Christine Macintyre)

Guess what, I am a special child,
I have a special Mum,
School makes me work hard all day long,
There's not much time for fun.
It will be worth it, I've been told,
One day I will be glad,
But it's today and I am young,
The pressure drives me mad.
My truly precious childhood years,
The best days so they say,
Spent catching up with boring stuff?
Please teacher, let me play!
For playing gives me so much joy,
I'm best at that, you see.
Why must I sit and learn strange things
That do not interest me?
Just let me play, that's how I'll learn
And then I'll make you proud.
I'll run and swim and learn to sing
And fly beyond the clouds!

(Christine Macintyre)

Activities

1. In what ways would/could you alter the curriculum for this 7-year-old?

2. What specific aims would you have?

The text sets out to meet the expectations of the Early Years Foundation Stage (EYFS) document, the Early Years Professional Status (EYPS) framework and the Curriculum for Excellence. These require practitioners to 'understand and appreciate the individual and diverse ways in which children develop and learn from birth to the end of the foundation stage'. The recommended way to do this is spelled out in the EYPS criterion, i.e. to 'use close, informed observations to monitor children's activity'.

Knowing how to support children's play is very hard. It must be based on perceptive observations; on understanding the children's perspective and developing eyes that can see all the opportunities for learning that are possible in play. Sometimes it means providing resources to match and extend the children's level of competence; often it means answering their questions in an open-ended way; and sometimes it means staying back so that the children can fulfil their ploys alone. Appreciating how and why and where and when is essential to getting it right.

Play provides a wonderful opportunity for observing and recording progress, for every aspect of children's development can be enhanced through play. And when adults become intrigued and engrossed they find that the rewards are so fulfilling, because through understanding the children's thinking, they are able to appreciate 'the colour of their dreams' (Dixon 2005).

And so this book has two key aims. The first is to support all those who wish to understand the complexities of children's play and find out how each aspect of their development (i.e. social, emotional, motor and intellectual) is enhanced through playing. That is done through analysing observations of children at play and recognising the learning that is there. The second is to provide study material for those who are seeking to gain new or further qualifications such as the Early Years Professional Status or different teaching qualifications, for example, the BA Early Years Education, the Early Years Foundation degree, the Early Childhood Studies degree and possibly the BTEC in Health and Social Care. All of these are based on studying children in the early years, finding out what it is that makes them fascinatingly different and finding out how to enhance their learning. Carrying out research, even small pieces of informal research such as carefully observing a few children at play in one setting, analysing and recording what they are learning and perhaps gathering pieces of their work as 'evidence' of claims, could make a significant contribution to an award, and so ideas of possible research topics are suggested throughout the text.

In each chapter there are pictures of children playing. These are not just lovely illustrations; they are there to stimulate and focus observations and expand recordings. The idea is that readers will study these, reflect on similar children in their own setting and, knowing how to analyse what they do, see them in a new light. When they do, they will be able to look at their children with more discerning eyes and provide many answers to Paley's (2004) stunning question, 'Who are you?'

There are developmental charts to allow comparisons of individual children's progress against recognised developmental norms and these can also be used to fire debates amongst professionals who may have different viewpoints based on their gathering conflicting data. There are diagrams that show what children could learn in various play scenarios, but of course these can be expanded and changed to suit specific places and different players. There are suggested activities that require adults to reflect and think about their own practice and in so doing remember the challenges that exist within play.

My hope is that everyone will be enriched by the effort of discovering more about children – for effort it requires! But of course that is one of the qualities of play too, and I hope the challenge of studying the children will be enjoyable as well as revealing and beneficial.

All these efforts will show parents, carers, practitioners and other professionals just how important studying play and keeping it as the focus of children's development is. We hope that all the adults caring for the children can share these aspirations and plans. If so, they can be reassured that their children are playing and learning just as well as they can. If 'others' have doubts and wish to reduce the time given to play, practitioners must be able to confidently justify the learning opportunities in a stress-free curriculum based on play. Then everyone will realise that all the outcomes of the Early Years documentation (EYFS and EYPS) and the Curriculum for Excellence *will* be achieved best of all through play.

To set the scene, take time to reflect on your own thoughts on play and consider your own answers to these fun questions, for play must be fun. Let's begin.

Do you play? If 'YES', what do you play at? Perhaps you enjoy going out to meet friends and chat? Perhaps you keep fit or play bridge or golf or climb mountains or just relax with a book? There are many things that could come under the umbrella term 'play' and many reasons for playing. Let's list a few.

Reasons for playing

Fun reasons – for enjoyment

Skill reasons – to improve an aspect of performance

Social reasons – to make or meet friends, the activity itself being less important

Fitness reasons – to maintain or improve health

Vertigo reasons – to challenge the environment and take the player nearly out of control, e.g. hang gliding, white water rafting

Cathartic reasons – playing to get release from stress elsewhere.

Activities

1. Think of the reasons why you play. Do different activities tick different boxes?

2. Discuss: Do children play for the same reasons or how do the reasons differ?

This activity highlights the point that children have different reasons for playing too, and understanding this is key to planning interventions. If children come to play primarily to meet friends or to join in a game of make believe and they are confronted by an adult who wishes to help them 'do better' in terms of skills they could improve, can you understand the confusion and resentment that could occur? So understanding children's reasons should precede intervention.

Perhaps as you play you feel great? Your endomorphins flow and you have a sense of satisfaction that carries you forward positively, even into the next day. You have made an independent choice about the things you like to do and carried it out. No one has suggested that it might be better if you practised something else – is that not true? Or perhaps your activity has not gone well and you are disappointed. What now? Well, you can either take a break or try again when you feel like it, or you can just abandon what you were doing, decide it's not for you and try something else. You might be a little disappointed but you won't feel you have failed.

And in these reflections, can we identify the characteristics of play? Let's try.

- freedom to choose what to do
- enjoyment in the activity
- independence in determining the pace and the level of challenge in the activity

- decision making about what to do and how long to do it
- no fear of failure, and
- above all, satisfaction in following your own wishes and ideas and finding that you have achieved something that perhaps you didn't realise you could do.

If these characteristics describe your play, surely we must ensure that children have many, many opportunities to experience them too? A little further reflection might reveal that these characteristics are at the root of many life choices such as what to study, where to work and possibly even when to leave home to become independent. Children at play might just be having a first try!

So adults must remember that when children play they are not setting out to discover something new or even to learn something, even though new learning will almost certainly be an incidental outcome of play. The children are making choices to suit what they want to do. They may use their imaginations and find magic in their fantasy play or they may choose a more practical venture and mould clay to enjoy the feeling of that medium or to discover what it can make. They may even share their concerns with a sympathetic listener. Three-year-old Tim, swirling water in the water tray, explained, 'That's how my tummy feels when I come in the morning.' And when Lauren, a new practitioner, said, 'Me too!', a bond was formed and they took comfort from each other. Three- and 4-year-old children may play with a friend and learn to share and to follow someone else's lead so that they can cooperate in and appreciate someone else's game. This is primarily important for their social development. And as they do this they are developing confidence in their own abilities, possibly empathising with others (emotional learning) and practising new skills (movement or motor learning). They are also learning by imitating their friends, a genuine form of intellectual learning. Are there things we can teach very young children that are more valuable than that? I wonder.

Activity

Discussion topic: Imitation

Think of the ways you learn from imitating someone else. Perhaps you imitated a colleague for a bit when you were new in the setting?

Perhaps you imitated what a child was doing to get him to open up and describe his plan?

Imitation is being recognised as an important learning strategy. Are there ways we could employ it more? What are they?

And if you don't play, if you say 'No' to the 'Do you play?' question, what do you do instead? Perhaps you have made a conscious decision to put away childish things or perhaps the pressure of work means you have no time to play? Or perhaps you enjoy your work so much that work and play have come together to provide the satisfaction and motivation you need to keep going?

It is interesting, and it takes our understanding forward, if we try to differentiate between play and work. In this example I have taken just one activity, reading a book, and I have set out the differences.

TABLE 0.1 Reading a book

PLAY	WORK	
Selecting a book	Chosen by the reader	Imposed on the reader
Language	The reader chooses the level of difficulty, readily understands the meaning	May be too difficult, e.g. with specialist terminology
Purpose	Enjoyment, relaxation	Extend knowledge
	To deepen interest in the chosen topic	Deepen understanding
Pace	Chosen by the reader	Must meet deadlines set elsewhere
Additional action	None. Can skim over text or miss parts	Memorising, analysing, criticising, linking theory to practice, evaluating
Tension	Can abandon book if unfinished	Must finish the set task and try to do it well

From my attempt to do this, you can see that 'freedom' and 'choice', i.e. to continue reading or not to trouble, are key characteristics of play. Important too are 'outside' expectations and the pressure which results from their fulfilment. In play there is no end product, no time pressure, and so there is no fear of failure. Moreover, because the activity is chosen by the players themselves, one can assume that it is pleasing to them; it is fun.

And of course there are children who do not wish to play or are unable to play. Could it be that they find the freedom overwhelmingly difficult? There are many children who can't make a choice or imagine what to play at or don't know how to join into a game. Play for them is hard work. How can we teach them how to play? Perhaps we should make suggestions as to what they might do and/or provide work activities, such as baking, first, so that they gain confidence in themselves and so develop the capacity to play? In so doing are we recognising that, for them, playing is harder than working? What do you think?

Such ideas and questions form the tenor of the book – that is, that play is a wonderful learning opportunity for children and that adults must be wary of intervening inappropriately, even taking over and so limiting the children by turning their play into work.

But at the same time they must recognise that children are all different and that being able to play is not easy for them all. Perhaps some children have not yet developed the competences that allow them to play without becoming aggressive or spoiling the play for others? Perhaps the gender differences between boys and girls or even the social conditioning from home are limiting their play choices? The physiological development that impacts on development and the burgeoning of emotional traits such as empathy and self-esteem are an important part of the book. All our children are from different social/cultural backgrounds and have already established ways of doing things. They are individuals, products of their nature and nurture, who need our understanding and support to become good players. Then they can experience the pleasure and satisfaction of experiencing something that is truly their own, something that will give them confidence and competence in the long educational journey they must make.

Activity

Choose one child that you care for. Consider the question 'Who are you?'. Make a list, then find what you can add when you have read the book.

Identifying Children's Learning in Different Episodes of Play

Chapter overview

This chapter sets out to show how learning is implicit in play from the very earliest times. It shares ideas on how to 'Plan and provide safe and appropriate child-led and adult initiated experiences, activities and play opportunities in indoor, outdoor and in out-of-setting contexts, which enable children to develop and learn' (EYPS criterion S11). It answers the questions that parents and child minders at home and practitioners in Families and Children's Centres, in Early Years Centres, in nurseries and playgroups ask about supporting the children in their care.

Q: When do young children actually begin to learn through play?

A: From birth, most parents will try to play with their baby, although in the earliest weeks the effort and the assessment are really made by the parents, with the baby being a fairly passive recipient of love and attention. But gradually the babies develop the strength to refine their random movements and the capacity to hold gaze and smile, and then true reciprocity can be seen. This gives pleasure to both and ensures that the game will go on. And go on it does in ever more sophisticated ways, using rhythm and language, imitation and repetition. In the first two pictures, Lilly shows this well. Cacioppo and Patrick (2008) explain that imitation is an innate competence that reinforces the neural pathways in the brain (see Chapter 4), contributing to intellectual development, development of movement, communication and synchrony. So monitoring children's capacity to imitate could make a very useful pointer for observation, and for children who cannot do this, introducing songs with simple actions – e.g. 'Fly away Peter, fly

---

away Paul' – could help them recognise what imitation is. Learning about or monitoring children's capacities for imitation might make a useful topic for further study/investigation.

When I saw these pictures I said 'wow' because Lilly and her parents clearly show how even early play experiences enhance and enchant learning.

Can you see how the processes of attachment and communication are being enhanced through playing 'round and round the garden' together? The faces of the players radiate involvement, joy and trust, such important indicators of social and emotional development, and alongside these there are other, perhaps more subtle, gains. For, in the first picture, as Lilly is being held aloft she is developing her spatial awareness. She is experiencing high and low and where she is in relation to her different surroundings as well as to her mother. She is seeing the world from another perspective – perhaps in her eyes a precarious one – and as she does so she is developing trust and successfully meeting a challenge. This contributes to her self-concept, an important part of her emotional development.

Then, in the second picture, look how accurately she points. Movements of the fingers like this are often clumsy in babies, who tend to use whole hand pats rather than differentiated pointing. Lilly's span indicates that she is strong enough to control her fingers even when she has stretched out wide. This is an important developmental observation because, in the baby/toddler, strength develops from head to toe (cephalo-caudal) and centre to periphery (proximo-distal). This explains why babies hold their heads up before they sit and sit before they stand and why reaching and grasping accurately comes after the development of core trunk strength. And as she holds herself erect, even as she tips to the side, Lilly is strengthening her whole body. She is learning about balance and coping with balance changes and so she is enhancing her movement or motor development, and this will stand her in good stead as she strives to achieve her motor milestones. (See Appendix 1.)

In the second picture, Lilly is stretching out to share the game with her father. She is showing that she has remembered the sequence of the jingle and is anxious to share her pleasure. She is also imitating her mother.

Moreover, when Lilly uses her fingertips like this, she is energising the frontal cortex of her brain where problem solving and the more sophisticated kinds of learning take place (Winkley 2004). This is because each fingertip is connected to a large piece of tissue there. So shared play activities, such as 'Five little buns in a baker's shop', do much more than teach counting. There are subtle gains that practitioners need to appreciate if they are to recognise all the learning potential in different play activities.

When Lilly stretches to the side, she is showing that she can adjust her balance, tipping over but not too far and then regaining her original safe position. This is challenging, yet we see her laughing, showing that she is confident and ready for more challenges like this. And of course the rhyme and the rhythm of the jingle are pleasing to Lilly and her parents. This is a simple, easily repeated jingle; it's something to share, and a timed pause heralding 'a tickely under there' often leads to laughter, repetition and more fun.

Look again at the picture of Lilly and her dad. The evident shared pleasure in the exchange reveals the bonding that will endure far, far beyond the game itself. Lewis (2000: 156) shows how most babies from a very early age are primed to detect emotionality in others and that this awareness 'provides the bedrock for the child's understanding of their own feelings'. This is a key example of emotional development. Robinson (2011: 49) explains further. She shows how this self-knowledge develops into the child beginning to empathise with the feelings of others. She writes, 'We cannot be attuned to someone else if we have not had the experience of someone being attuned to us.' The picture shows how the play has allowed a high level of attunement between Lilly and her parents.

So observations need to consider the whole child in each specific environment to gain a comprehensive picture of what is really going on. Play episodes, even very early ones like this, hold great potential for emotional, social and motor development. And as Lilly remembers this game, easily seen as she anticipates it with pleasure next time round, then there are intellectual, memorising and sequencing gains too.

Activity

Before you read on, list Lilly's learning under the headings 'social', 'emotional', 'motor' and 'intellectual'.

Now compare your list to the one below.

TABLE 1.1 Summary of learning gains from playing 'Round and round the garden'

SOCIAL LEARNING	EMOTIONAL LEARNING	MOTOR LEARNING	INTELLECTUAL LEARNING
Playing together encourages socialising and turn taking. These are precursors to language and to interpreting non-verbal communication, i.e. appreciating what others are thinking and feeling without talking. This is the basis of empathy and altruism.	Observers know that Lilly can appreciate the rhythm of the jingle by her anticipating the ending – possibly curling up to avoid the tickle. She gains confidence from Mum and Dad's participation and enjoyment of the game. She is in charge!	Balance practice as Lilly adjusts her position to allow stretching out without toppling over. Pointing practice develops finger awareness and, in this case, spatial awareness.	Appreciation of the rhyme and rhythm of the jingle. Memorising the sequence of the words. Fingertip practice energising the frontal cortex, the executive thinking area in the cerebral cortex of the brain.

Organising observations

Observing children at play and analysing what is being learned needs a great deal of practice and patience in the early stages, but it does lead to making more meaningful recordings that endure over time so that progress can be accurately monitored. This would be vital if any developmental delay was suspected, for the question, 'When did you first notice . . .', will certainly be asked. Observations are made even more difficult by the overwhelming number of different activities children choose to do. But there is a bonus, for Vygotsky (1978) showed that the study of play and that of child development naturally complement each other. He claimed that, '*As in the focus of a magnifying glass, play contains all the developmental tendencies in a condensed form.*' And because it does, it is helpful to have a structure that can make this complex study more manageable. The one suggested here is to subdivide the study of development into four aspects, namely:

- Social development, or the study of how children build relationships and learn to interact in groups
- Motor development, or the study of how children learn to move efficiently and effectively in different environments
- Intellectual or cognitive development, or the study of how children learn to be logical and rational thinkers
- Emotional or affective development, or the study of how children's feelings and perceptions affect their behaviour and learning.

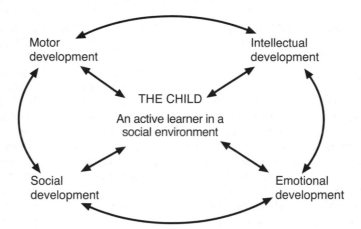

The diagram shows that the child is a social being in a complex environment. The child enacts on the environment and is affected by it – hence the nature/nurture effect that impacts on every aspect of development.

Q: Is one aspect of development more important than the others?

Social development

Many parents and teachers would say that the social dimension of learning is the most important one because if children are happy they are likely to be more receptive and confident and therefore more able to interact with their peers *and* take new learning on board, or at least they will not be afraid to ask for help. Vygotsky's (1978) concept of 'the zone of proximal development' and Bruner's (1966) idea of 'scaffolding' both claim that if children are supported by more knowledgeable others as they learn – and these need only be one step ahead – they will be able to move forward more quickly than if they tried to learn alone. Social interaction with adults and peers is therefore vitally important because it enables children to:

- Learn how to make and keep a friend
- Imitate, copy and show others, and so share their learning
- Interact appropriately with adults and other children
- Cooperate in group situations
- Take the lead role in decision making and at other times conform in the subsidiary role
- Become aware that others also have needs
- Learn to empathise, i.e. understand different perspectives
- Understand how events affect others
- Develop/recognise socially acceptable behaviour in different circumstances
- Make decisions (social and/or moral) and stay with them
- Develop altruism, i.e. caring for others at some cost to oneself.

Motor development

The motor aspects of development concern the acquisition of practical skills through developing abilities such as balance, coordination, strength and speed of movement. The underlying skills of planning movements so that they are efficient and effective involve much perceptual learning based on making balance and kinaesthetic (spatial) decisions. These depend on the other senses (i.e. visual, auditory and tactile) interpreting environmental cues accurately, so that feedback into the sensory system guides decisions about when to move, what to move and where to go.

Large movements involving the large muscle groups are known as gross motor skills while the smaller muscle groups contribute to fine motor control.

NB If children have a learning difficulty, it can often be spotted first in poor balance and poor movement coordination. Floppiness, indicating poor muscle strength, should always be noted and, if it persists, physiotherapy help should be sought without delay.

It is vital that due attention is given to motor development, because 'movement is a child's first language' and because it enables children to:

- Control their movements with increasing dexterity
- Move effectively and safely in different environments
- Develop spatial and kinaesthetic awareness
- Develop the abilities that underlie skilled performance, i.e. balance, coordination and control
- Know how to organise sequences of movement
- Become involved in healthy activities
- Enjoy participating in activities and games
- Become confident in tackling new movement challenges.

Intellectual development

The intellectual or cognitive aspects of development concern the acquisition of knowledge and understanding about all aspects of everyday life and all the appropriate activities of daily living. Parents and professionals are often (in my view) overly concerned to have their children count and write their name far too early because attempting to do so before they have the neurological development to do so could cause stress or even lasting harm. There are so many more useful things to learn and so many problems to solve, for this aspect of development helps children to:

- Develop knowledge and understanding of the world
- Set themselves problems, e.g. 'How do I empty this cupboard?' or 'How do I put a disk in the computer?'
- Understand ordering and sequencing, e.g. 'I put my socks on before my boots' or 'I must pay for sweets at the checkout before I eat them'
- Develop language and communication skills
- Develop the capacity to think logically and rationally, e.g. 'If I do this then that is likely to happen'
- Develop mathematical, literacy and scientific concepts through play activities
- Think creatively about new ways of doing things
- Concentrate on the task at hand
- Contribute to fantasy play.

Emotional development

This is perhaps the most difficult area to understand, possibly because the development of confidence, as one example, is only apparent in carrying out another task or perhaps in changed non-verbal behaviour, which is always difficult to assess. Competences such as appreciation or imagination are less tangible than, for example, getting a sum right and making progress in mathematics, but this is a hugely important aspect of development because it allows children to:

- Pretend to be someone else and so be involved in role-play
- Approach new situations with confidence
- Share/express feelings and emotions
- Cope with anxieties and be more resilient when things go wrong
- Confront open-ended problems and find solutions
- Enjoy art/music/dance, i.e. the creative aspects of development
- Cry if they want to
- Understand that others may have different ideas
- Appreciate the value of friendship
- Develop altruism or caring for someone who is hurt
- Appreciate the atmosphere, e.g. in a church
- Be innovative and imaginative.

As all of this terminology becomes clear, there are two other very important factors to remember. First, one aspect of change may be dominant at one time and affect the others. Think of the previously biddable 2-year-old who suddenly wants his own way all of the time and has tantrums whenever he is thwarted. Frustration has taken over because he has not developed the language to make his wishes known or the 'nous' to recognise how inappropriate his intentions are!

Parents and practitioners also have to remember that going to a new setting is a huge challenge, particularly for only children who have not had to share toys and who have had unlimited access to mum. Now 'she has disappeared'. Moreover the setting may have rules and boundaries quite different from those at home. Is it any wonder that the child regresses and functions as a younger child? Not speaking, wetting pants or being aggressive may just be ways of showing distress.

Q: You said that gains in one aspect of development permeate into the others. Can you give an example of how they interact?

Case study

Let's think about 5-year-old Gordon who has just learned to swim. He has made a huge stride in the motor aspect of his development. He has learned about balance, coordination, rhythm and control, but progress here also spills over into the other areas. Now that he is able to swim, he can join his swimming friends, a social gain; he has learned the names of different strokes and when they are best used and the properties of water in terms of floating, sinking and buoyancy, i.e. intellectual gains; and he may sympathise with other non-swimming children and seek to help them, i.e. social/emotional gains. Possibly best of all, as he has become more confident in his own ability to learn a new skill, his self-esteem has been boosted and this is a vital emotional gain.

The arrows in Figure 1.3 (p. 11) linking the different subdivisions of development are there to remind those who observe children, assess their progress and plan learning activities on that basis, that progress in one area is likely to benefit other areas as well. In a similar vein, new or unhappy experiences can cause children to regress to an earlier developmental stage in each aspect. Then they will appear unable to do something that they had mastered before. This explains why parents can be flummoxed to find that their toilet-trained youngster has been having accidents in his nursery. His changing lifestyle has caused him to regress. He only needs time and calm to re-establish himself in new surroundings. Recognising this can meet the EYPS criterion SO3, i.e. 'How children's well being, development, learning and behaviour can be affected by a range of influences from inside and outside the setting.'

Difficulties in recording

This interplay means that at times it can be difficult to know where to place different observations. If a child is able to get dressed putting his clothes on in the correct order when previously that was really difficult, what kind of progress is that? Is it intellectual? (The child has learned that pants go on before trousers and that trousers should be done up.) Is it motor? (The child has now developed the fine motor coordination to be able to do up buttons and tie laces.) Is it emotional? (The child has gained confidence from becoming more independent.) In my view, considering progress across the spectrum is more important than recording observations in the 'correct' place.

NB Considering the four headings means that one aspect is not omitted during the observations. It may be that close observation in one aspect is only possible on one day but that can be followed by monitoring the effect on the other aspects the next. In that way a comprehensive picture of development is gained.

Sometimes, just as different people have different reasons for doing things, so children can put the greatest value on the less obvious benefits, e.g. 'When I can swim I'll be allowed to go to the pool without Mum.' This child is eager to be free. So observations can be enriched by listening too.

It is particularly important to listen to children's speech and monitor how it is developing. Poor articulation can be a sign of poor muscle tone in the mouth, and singing and having chewy items at snack time can help. But continued delay needs expert support by a speech and language therapist. Along with articulation, practitioners should monitor comprehension to find out if the children really understand what is being said. This can be gleaned by observing their reaction in shared conversations, for sometimes children with clear and fluent speech do not understand what they say.

This is hyperlexia and should be an immediate cause for concern. So should disappearing speech. When children who have spoken even a few words can no longer do so, this must be recorded and immediate help sought, as this *might* be a sign of autism. But of course no hint of this should be shared with the parents until expert advice from a psychologist has been given. It can be difficult in some regions to get outside expert advice, but many difficulties do not go away and early expert intervention is essential.

Let's take some nursery examples now and analyse what children are learning. Let's enjoy some dancing.

The 4-year-olds in the picture, Katie and Leah, have reached the developmental stage of playing together and enjoying same-sex friendships.

Q: But what are they learning?

A: The answer to this is subdivided into the four aspects of development, as before. The girls are gaining:

■ Emotional learning

They are enjoying having a friend and cooperating to produce a dance together. And in dressing up to fit the part, their role-play allows them to become real dancers. They are developing the expressive side of their imaginative work. They are gaining confidence and satisfaction from experiencing the twirling of the dance and building something they can show to other children. They are also expressing their pleasure and their freedom in composing the dance steps. The dance is theirs.

■ Social learning

The girls have to discuss what to do and possibly have their own ideas overturned. So they are involved in a give and take scenario, a valuable learning experience. They are also planning to show their dance to friends and no doubt they will chat to others and share their enjoyment.

■ Motor learning

The children are strengthening their arms as they pull to make the turns flow and they are responding to the rhythm of the movement. They are depending on each other to hold their balance and judging the size of the steps that will take them round in time to the music. How they cope with the rhythm is a critically important observation, for many children later found to have dyslexia/dyspraxia tend to avoid rhythmical experiences.

■ Intellectual learning

The girls have to remember the sequence of their dance steps and how they fit the music. These children actually made their 'twirling dance' after seeing falling leaves so their language developed too. They also listened to several pieces of music to find one 'that was all twirly'. So their musical appreciation skills were enhanced.

Moreover in all of this, they persevered until their dance was ready. They discussed where they would dance (this necessitated asking others – politely – to move out of the way), what music they would have and where it could be played, what costumes would be suitable – 'we want dresses that match' – and in consultation with their teacher, they organised when and how they could show their dance to their friends.

Activity

Think of a play activity like this that you have observed in your own setting. Analyse it using the four headings.

Which category was hardest to write? Why do you think this was?

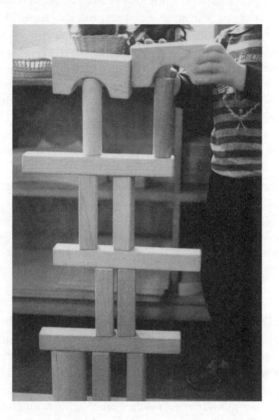

Let's find now what Ryan is doing and plan observations around that.

Q: I can appreciate that Ryan must be concentrating hard as he builds his tower. What is he learning?

A: Let's listen to David. He is a young man who is in charge of a small group of children. He is studying for an Early Years BA degree. He made this analysis. As you read, think of the subdivision and think if you could have added any more information. At a study group, David, who had taken the picture as Ryan built his tower, explained as follows.

Case study

The first and most obvious observation to record is that Ryan is totally immersed in building his tower. His concentration is fantastic when there's any mention of construction – diggers, holes in the ground, laying pipes. These are his over-riding interests. He's had several previous attempts at building but this is the most successful. The strange thing is that when a previous tower collapsed at level two, he rebuilt levels one and two as they were even though they weren't very stable. I would like some advice on whether I should have intervened at that point. How long do you let children struggle? But I felt that his increased concentration and remembering showed intellectual gains.

His fine motor skills were amazing I thought. You can see that he is using two hands to do different things at the midline and he is very gentle in placing the bricks. Actually he is taking the top brick away as he has realised it won't balance. He has terrific control. He is standing well balanced at the correct distance from the tower and moving very slowly. So I would consider that a high level of motor learning.

Socially Ryan is a loner. He is not unpleasant to the other children but he won't let them join his game; he just doesn't want to play. And activities like this don't encourage cooperating with another child. But play is all about giving choices. Emotionally he is getting a great deal of satisfaction; he is content and he'll have to cope with disappointment when his tower collapses. That's all I have to say.

To foster Ryan's social skills, David decided to have some building with real bricks outside in the yard. He showed them to Ryan and another child who had enjoyed making roads in the sand using toy diggers. Would the shared interest help them to work together? Sadly the answer was 'No.' Ryan stayed for a short time then raced back to the indoor bricks. David was concerned – was this a deep interest or an obsession? He monitored Ryan using a time sampling frame to gather proof of how much time Ryan spent with his bricks despite efforts to interest him in other things. Later he passed this 'evidence' to a psychologist. Happily once Ryan gained confidence he was gradually able to join in, but his way of dealing with any upset was to retreat to building his bricks once again.

David's question about intervention was tantalising. What do you think? Should he have 'sorted' the bricks so that the balance was better? How do you think Ryan would have reacted? (Chapter 2 deals with intervention.)

Sometimes ideas for study can be stimulated by a photograph or a drawing or just by something a child has said. When 4-year-old Elena, throwing autumn leaves into the sky, announced, 'When these leaves go up to heaven they paint the rainbows', some of the children had such fun painting wonderful rainbows, full of colour and flowers. And later they discussed real rainbows, but abandoned this, preferring to build 'a yellow brick road'.

A nursery nurse in the same setting explained her predicament in recording observations:

> About five of the older children got themselves into a game in the garden but it was difficult to hear what they were saying. I didn't want to go too close in case I spoiled the play. The television was showing 'Dorothy' and the yellow brick road had given them the idea that they could go somewhere over the rainbow. The three boys gathered stones to make the road and the girls went inside to the dressing-up box to find costumes.
>
> There was a bit of disagreement then because the girls seemed to follow the storyline but the boys were more interested in 'making a good road'. I did hear that. Unfortunately the play died away after that, however we recorded it as an example of group fantasy play.

It can be frustrating to know that children have moved up to the stage of fantasising and not be able to record what they are saying. Jade did well to stay back but was disappointed to see the play fizzle out because of the sudden switch of interests, but she respected the children's choice.

Play as the best way to educate children

Q: I understand about learning through play now, but what about play itself? I see children playing every day and they are all doing different things. They are always busy and rarely bored or grizzly but I just thought it was something children did – I never thought to describe it or to have to justify it as part of a curriculum. But that's what I need to do now. I remember reading somewhere that we shouldn't even begin to try to describe play, indeed that trying to do so was like trying to catch the wind in a paper bag and I thought how good that was – it captured the ethereal nature of play – but it didn't really help me to spell out exactly what play was and I need to be able to do that to justify what I am doing in promoting play. So what *is* it?

A: There have been many authors who try to define play. They claim that children do not differentiate between play and work and agree with Paley (2004) that 'Play is a child's work.' The best definition for me, however, has always been the one written by Susan Isaacs in 1933. She gave us a wonderfully revealing description of play that has stood the test of time. She wrote,

Play is a child's life and the means by which he comes to understand the world around him.

So if play is a child's life, surely it should be composed of a variety of happy experiences that engender confidence and self-belief and interactions where the children build a composite, realistic and happy picture of themselves. This will allow them to build a positive self-esteem, or later when they come to appreciate how others are thinking and feeling, a theory of mind. Researchers such as Bee and Boyd (2005) are convinced that this understanding of oneself is essential to beginning to appreciate and assess the attributes of others. Play experiences provide a basis for developing understanding and for fostering the skills that are necessary to move, to plan, to act and to learn from a new experience. Surely no one would deny that that is real learning?

Isaacs' brief but comprehensive definition encompasses all the different kinds of activities children choose to do and the opportunities they have to learn. It explains that children come to understand their world (or in other words, all the happenings in their family and then in their wider culture or environment) through play activities. And these activities should be explored and practised at a pace that matches the children's wishes and stage of maturation. In the early years especially, play activities are best undertaken for their own sake. They are not goal-directed. The children are not setting out to learn particular things or to practise skills that could be useful in the future. Young children are intrigued by participating in the here and now, that is by being children. The learning that occurs is implicit in the activity. This may gradually change as children begin to formulate plans and make things or set out to become more skilled at particular tasks. But if they are left in charge, then these activities can still be called play. Once adults take over, once there is a shift in responsibility and ownership, once children wait for adults to suggest the next step or 'something they might make', the opportunities for the children's own fantasy play are reduced. So the experience is no longer childlike. The danger then is that play becomes tedious work.

Q: So what are children doing as they play?

A: Young children especially are playing to find out, to investigate rather than to practise, and so achievements are multifaceted and transitory. And if things don't work out they can walk away.

Adults have to know how to analyse what the children are learning and this means recognising all the underlying skills and making them explicit. Only then can they show doubters that play activities allow children to achieve the skills and competences that will enable rich learning now and provide a sound basis for the future when greater demands are made. But we must acknowledge that childhood is a precious time in its own right. It is not a preparation time for later. The author, teacher, artist and poet Peter Dixon (2005) urges those who do not believe this, to get out a zimmer and practise now.

And when we consider different kinds of play, because these change as part of a natural developmental sequence as well as the children having greater experience, we discover that Isaacs' description could fit play activities for any age group. For children's play begins soon after birth as adults observe them and initiate the process of communication and attachment. And soon, adults and children together initiate language play, perhaps through 'cooing' or using the gentle, rhythmic tones of motherese or, as it is now called, infant-directed speech. This encourages even new babies to hold gaze (the beginnings of attachment and communication) and even momentarily attempt to respond. Surely these early interactions are a kind of play? They certainly fit all the criteria of choice and freedom and learning. If you doubt this, watch a disenchanted baby ignore efforts to engage him.

So if we were to provide some descriptive words for play, would 'exploration, discovery, freedom, fulfilment, excitement, satisfaction and joy' be best? These would keep the ethereal nature of play and its magic alive.

The changing nature of children's play

Q: In the play episodes you have described and from my observations, I noticed that very young children mostly play alone. They do their own thing and don't seem interested in anyone else. Then they begin to want a friend . . . so social learning becomes more important. Why is that?

A: As babies become toddlers and toddlers become children, they gain competence in all aspects of their development. These developing capacities together with various and varied experiences of the environment allow them to increase the number of things they can do. And so it is with play. And as they grow, children play at different things. Researchers who have studied these differences (Piaget and Inhelder 1969; Rubin *et al.* 1983) have found that free play progresses in a pre-determined way. Although it could be misleading to call these differences 'stages', as the behaviours mingle and mix rather than change abruptly, there are qualitative differences in the types of play which children exhibit as they grow older and these are now described.

Sensorimotor play

At around 4 months, children play with their hands, their first toy. They are fascinated by the patterns they make and gradually realise two things. The first is that these hands belong to them and they have some control over them; the second is that they can be used to hit and then grasp objects that are out there in space. These early movement patterns are very important in developing coordination and efficient movement. As babies reach out to grasp they are making spatial decisions, e.g. how far do I reach and in what direction? Timing ones, e.g. when do I open my hand to grasp? And when do I let go? Speed ones, e.g. how fast do I need to move? And body boundary ones: where do I end and where does the toy begin? The children are developing coordination through these early movements which when practised will become habitual and automatic. Through all of this playful activity, which needs sustained concentration, the children are building 'practical intelligence', i.e. a store of skills, which will form the basis of a repertoire of many more advanced movements.

Slightly later, when grasping has been achieved, babies discover the properties of objects by sucking them, as the mouth is very sensitive and conveys messages of hardness or softness or different tastes. In all of this exploratory play, the baby, without any tutoring, is learning what objects can do and is learning to handle them with increasing dexterity. Later still, at 9 months or so, the ability to crawl opens up a new play vista. Toys can be retrieved, taken to another place or moved along the floor. Cupboards formerly out of range can be reached and emptied – the contents providing lots of problem-solving activities – although the problem of fitting them back into place is usually ignored.

Constructive play

By 18 months children enjoy building with bricks and knocking the edifice down. They replace the bricks with increasing dexterity, using the fingers and thumb, i.e. a pincer grip to grasp rather than the whole hand which makes letting go difficult.

They enjoy repetitive play and anticipating the same surprise, as in peek-a-boo games. They begin to show interest in simple puzzles such as inset boards or five-piece jigsaws and they will applaud any that are completed. At 2 years plus, they will make snakes with play-dough. At this stage, toys are used for their real purpose, a spoon is a spoon.

Symbolic play

Between 2 and 3 years, children use one object to represent another. Their developing imaginations allow them to pretend for example that a wooden brick is a car and they will drive the brick along the pretend road with accompanying realistic noises. At this stage children stay immersed in their games for a longer spell because they have the physical ability to move around and many more ideas about what different objects do. Just as they can now pretend or imagine one thing is something else, they also begin to pretend that they themselves are other people – this is the start of role-play.

At age 2, children also begin to play 'in parallel' rather than in the solitary way they did earlier. This means that they will play alongside other children, making occasional contact with them, e.g. briefly showing interest in what they are doing or moving towards them to share their own play. These communications gradually lengthen and lead to children playing together, perhaps engaging in cooperative role-play. This usually appears earlier in siblings who share the same stories and other experiences.

Sociodramatic play

Three- and 4-year-old children, who now play together rather than alone, now enact all the roles they see around them and demonstrate detailed understanding of their perceptions of mummy, daddy and baby, doctor, nurse and patient, and even characters in their favourite stories. Often a great deal of time can be taken up in allocating and rejecting parts to the detriment of the real game ever beginning at all. The smallest children are very often given the 'baddie' parts because they are the ones who do not fully understand the character of the role they have to play – or it may be the only way they are allowed to join in – or they may not have the language it takes to refuse. At this age the dominant players in a group of children are emerging. It is best if the same ones do not lead all of the time.

This is the time when many children have imaginary companions and give them a special role as friend or dog or whatever. For a time these friends are very real to the children and seem to support them just as a pet does. Adults can feel strange having to search for lost imaginary friends or having to set a place for them at table, but they can be reassured that this phase will pass for it is a normal part of the development of pretence (Taylor 1993). An imaginary friend, who of course always agrees and who makes no demands, can help the child, providing a secure base, almost a retreat, so that the worries of the day can be shared. The 'friend' can also make comments that the child is wary of putting forward, and, when the suggestion misfires, take the blame.

Case study

My own daughter had an imaginary best friend, 'Jane'. She came everywhere – we had to be careful not to sit on her in the car and she had her own set of eating likes and dislikes that were listed regularly. Moreover, she was usually blamed for any mishap, 'Must've been Jane', and sometimes she was used as a shelter, 'Jane says she's not going to do that . . .' or 'Jane's a silly girl to want the light on, but she does.' One day a scream from the back of the car nearly had us in a ditch. The scream was because 'Jane has been left in Dindal' (Dingwall, a holiday place 200 miles distant). The fact that we couldn't return to collect her was met by howls and heartbreaking sobs until we had the brainwave to say we'd pick her up at the airport. Jane lasted for months but suddenly we realised she had disappeared. Maybe the child had grown confident enough to cope on her own?

Any kind of role-playing can help develop altruism, i.e. caring for someone else at some cost to yourself, as children, taking the part of a parent or a nurse, begin to appreciate the demands of that role. In this way they may become less self-centred and see the world from the viewpoint of another person – they move from being egocentric to becoming sociocentric. This is important social learning in helping them move into a wider society.

An important change happens when 5- and 6-year-olds become able to plan ahead. Now they can indicate what game will be played and visualise a sequence of events even up to deciding how the game will end. Tears and battles can occur if not all of the players understand the proposed sequences or agree with them. Indeed the planners may expect others to share their understanding without ever having explained what the game was about at all. For children who cannot empathise and understand that others may have different views, playing can be confusing indeed.

Games with rules

Very often the rules of games are not explained to novice players; they are learned by playing the game. Very early games have simple rules – the adult in the peek-a boo game will demonstrate carefully what is to happen and play patiently till the baby understands. As the games become more complex, the first-time player can have a difficult time observing and understanding the rules. In a game of 'I spy with my little eye', a 4-year-old had a wonderful time disclaiming the efforts of her older friends who guessed everything imaginable for the letter 'W'. When they eventually gave in and asked for the solution, the child looked blank – no one had explained that she had to have identified an object beginning with 'W' herself. Did anyone ever explain that to you?

Interestingly, as the spontaneous games of the early years disappear and are replaced by 'recognised' games, e.g. rounders, card games or board games, the rules are made explicit on paper, although young children often adapt the game, e.g. snakes and ladders or Monopoly, to suit their own level of understanding. Playing is much more complex now and winning emerges as a new goal. Now children must learn the rules and practise the moves if they are to get better at playing.

And so there are many kinds of play, differing in the resources and the amount of structure provided by adults. As a result, children have variety and stimulation and so are enabled to learn many things. In structuring play activities and by carefully supporting children, adults hope that the benefits of play can be retained as more formal learning is introduced.

Through different kinds of play, children can experiment in a safe environment:

- To find: how things work, the effect altering one thing has on another, e.g. what happens to ice in warm water, the different properties of materials, e.g. wet and dry sand, and how these affect building; how different materials make different sounds; what kind of planning is necessary to accomplish a task.

- To understand: the responsibilities different people have, e.g. fireman, nurse, parents, and how they carry out their jobs; how different children react to being involved in a game, e.g. one child might smack a doll as punishment, even though she may not have been smacked herself. Another could be horrified by this response. Both learn that different people have different perceptions/ideas/evaluations.

- To imagine: scenes they have not experienced, e.g. meeting a friendly alien and travelling to his land; how stories could be enacted, and what different outcomes might be; how others feel in their role, e.g. as dancers on stage or television.

- To create: models, e.g. of castles in the wet sand; collages, e.g. using materials or sticky paper to make a scene; gifts for home, using threading or weaving or gluing.

- To act out: their own worries in a sheltered environment, e.g. going into hospital or sharing their toys with a new baby.

To derive full benefit from all these possibilities, adults need to provide the time, the resources and sometimes the ideas to start the children off or help them continue. In this way their learning can be extended in a myriad of ways and all through play.

The chapter now finishes by offering a range of play activities divided into possible social, emotional, intellectual and motor gains. These are to help planning and justifying play as the best thing children can do.

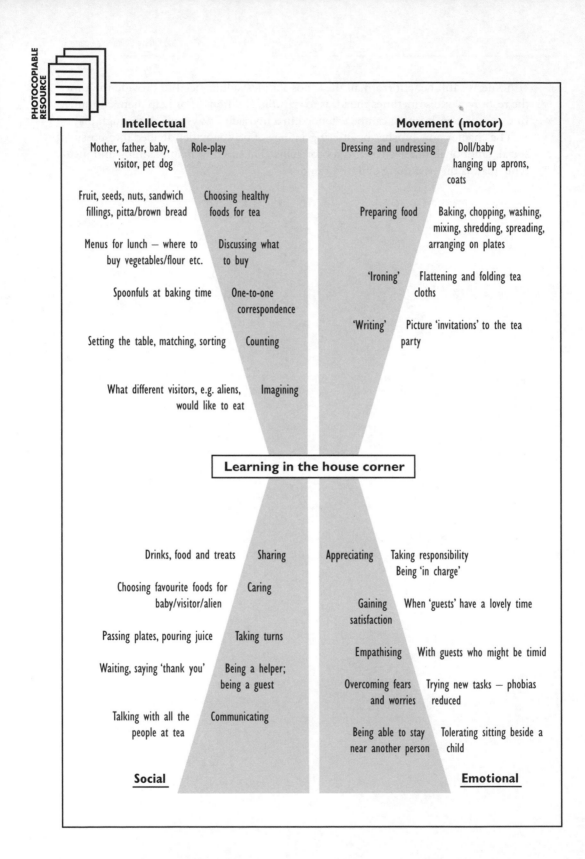

Intellectual

Mother, father, baby, visitor, pet dog — Role-play

Fruit, seeds, nuts, sandwich fillings, pitta/brown bread — Choosing healthy foods for tea

Menus for lunch — where to buy vegetables/flour etc. — Discussing what to buy

Spoonfuls at baking time — One-to-one correspondence

Setting the table, matching, sorting — Counting

What different visitors, e.g. aliens, would like to eat — Imagining

Movement (motor)

Dressing and undressing — Doll/baby hanging up aprons, coats

Preparing food — Baking, chopping, washing, mixing, shredding, spreading, arranging on plates

'Ironing' — Flattening and folding tea cloths

'Writing' — Picture 'invitations' to the tea party

Learning in the house corner

Drinks, food and treats — Sharing

Choosing favourite foods for baby/visitor/alien — Caring

Passing plates, pouring juice — Taking turns

Waiting, saying 'thank you' — Being a helper; being a guest

Talking with all the people at tea — Communicating

Appreciating — Taking responsibility
Being 'in charge'

Gaining satisfaction — When 'guests' have a lovely time

Empathising — With guests who might be timid

Overcoming fears and worries — Trying new tasks — phobias reduced

Being able to stay near another person — Tolerating sitting beside a child

Social

Emotional

from: *Enhancing Learning through Play*, Routledge © 2012 Christine Macintyre

Intellectual

Understanding that clothes can change characters — Role-playing

What shall I be? — Decision making

Will the costume fit? — Problem solving

Taking part in dramatic play, e.g. being a fireman — Acting

What resources will match my costume? — Planning

Movement (motor)

Dressing and changing clothes — Fastening buttons, zips

Using resources — Floor mop (Cinderella), tutu (ballet dancer)

Making resources — Crowns, necklaces, wands and other props

Learning in the dressing-up corner

Listening to their wishes — understanding perspective — Assisting others to dress up

(a) In waiting for a costume
(b) In building a drama sequence — Turn-taking

That characters change, and altering motivations to suit — Understanding

Someone else's ideas/plan and giving praise — Following and adapting ploys

Having confidence — (a) To join in (b) To become someone else and take on their role

Empathising

Understanding different roles

Avoiding suppressing fears — By acting them out in a safe place

Gaining satisfaction — From taking on another preferred role

Social

Emotional

from: *Enhancing Learning through Play*, Routledge © 2012 Christine Macintyre

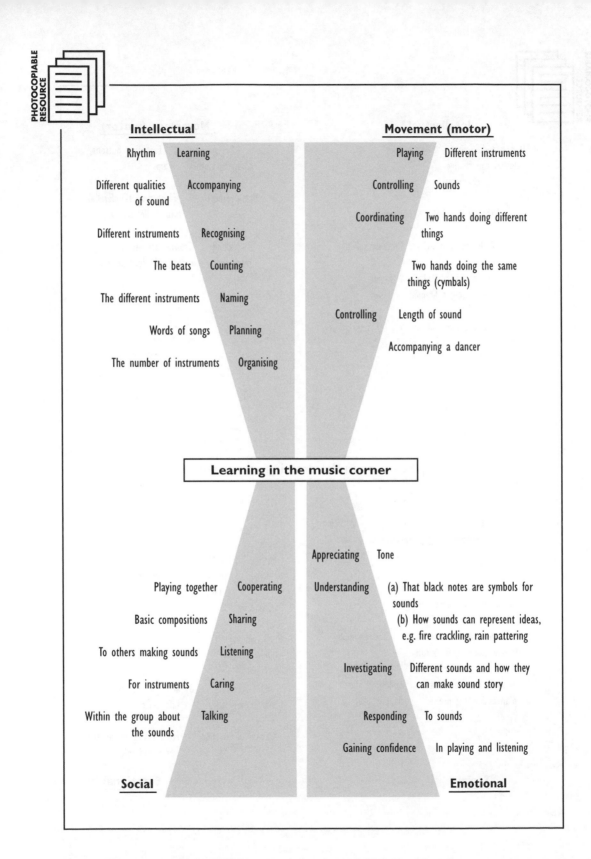

Intellectual

Rhythm   Learning

Different qualities   Accompanying
of sound

Different instruments   Recognising

The beats   Counting

The different instruments   Naming

Words of songs   Planning

The number of instruments   Organising

Movement (motor)

Playing   Different instruments

Controlling   Sounds

Coordinating   Two hands doing different
things

Two hands doing the same
things (cymbals)

Controlling   Length of sound

Accompanying a dancer

Learning in the music corner

Playing together   Cooperating

Basic compositions   Sharing

To others making sounds   Listening

For instruments   Caring

Within the group about   Talking
the sounds

Appreciating   Tone

Understanding   (a) That black notes are symbols for
sounds
(b) How sounds can represent ideas,
e.g. fire crackling, rain pattering

Investigating   Different sounds and how they
can make sound story

Responding   To sounds

Gaining confidence   In playing and listening

Social

Emotional

from: *Enhancing Learning through Play*, Routledge © 2012 Christine Macintyre

Intellectual

The sequence of actions — **Planning**

Equipment and resources — **Organising**

Remembering what comes first then next — **Sequencing**

Completing the action — **Doing**

Estimating distances/heights — **Judging**

Knowing when to jump, throw, chase etc. — **Timing**

Movement (motor)

Balancing — On benches before and after jumping

Coordinating actions, control — Slowing down and stopping at the correct time

Transitions — Joining two actions together

Gross motor skills — Crawling, climbing, walking, running, jumping, rolling*

*pencil rolls only for children with Down's syndrome

Outdoor play on large apparatus

Learning to let others go first (developing understanding of how others feel) — **Waiting Taking turns**

Watching others; copying good ideas on seesaw — **Cooperating**

Ball skills, e.g. throwing/catching/aiming — **Being part of a team**

Matching movements; fitting in spaces — **Making up a movement game in twos**

Paying attention — Remembering and carrying out instructions

Gaining confidence — Becoming motivated to try more movement sequences

Endorphins working

Releasing tension/energy/stress — Running, jumping, wheeling

Reducing cortisol — Calming down

Social

Emotional

from: *Enhancing Learning through Play*, Routledge © 2012 Christine Macintyre

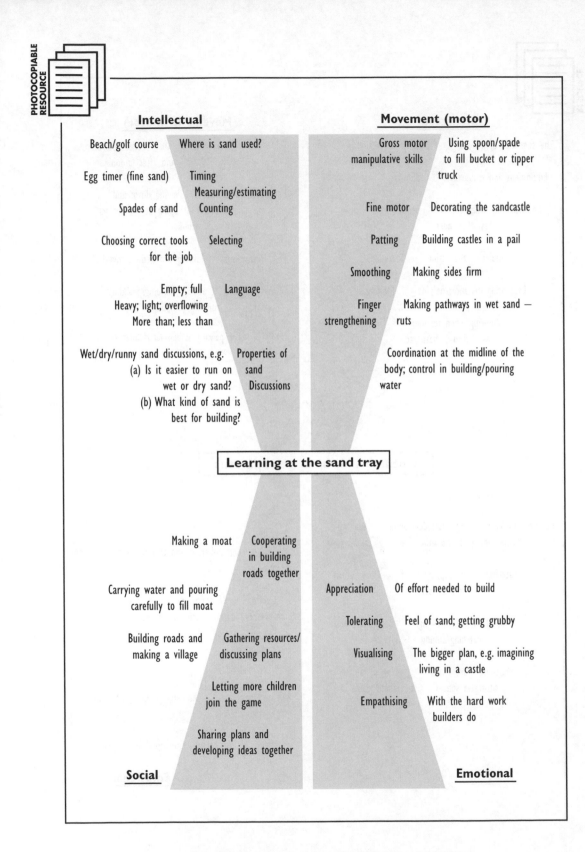

Intellectual

Beach/golf course   Where is sand used?

Egg timer (fine sand)   Timing
   Measuring/estimating
Spades of sand   Counting

Choosing correct tools   Selecting
for the job

Empty; full   Language
Heavy; light; overflowing
More than; less than

Wet/dry/runny sand discussions, e.g.   Properties of
(a) Is it easier to run on   sand
    wet or dry sand?   Discussions
(b) What kind of sand is
    best for building?

Movement (motor)

Gross motor   Using spoon/spade
manipulative skills   to fill bucket or tipper
   truck

Fine motor   Decorating the sandcastle

Patting   Building castles in a pail

Smoothing   Making sides firm

Finger   Making pathways in wet sand —
strengthening   ruts

Coordination at the midline of the
body; control in building/pouring
water

Learning at the sand tray

Making a moat   Cooperating
in building
roads together

Carrying water and pouring
carefully to fill moat

Building roads and   Gathering resources/
making a village   discussing plans

Letting more children
join the game

Sharing plans and
developing ideas together

Social

Appreciation   Of effort needed to build

Tolerating   Feel of sand; getting grubby

Visualising   The bigger plan, e.g. imagining
living in a castle

Empathising   With the hard work
builders do

Emotional

from: *Enhancing Learning through Play*, Routledge © 2012 Christine Macintyre

Intellectual

Building a cave that won't collapse; or a paper boat that will float in the moat

Learning about floating and sinking

Problem solving

Dry and wet sand — selecting and adapting

Estimating levels; pailfuls needed

Of water/ice/freezing melting disappearing

Understanding changing properties

Displacement of water when blocks are added to the tray; submerging

Floating and sinking

Investigating

Movement (motor)

Placing — Small world figures

Controlling — Water flow in filling/emptying tubes, syphons

Building — Wet sand; strengthening hands, arms and shoulders

Developing coordination at the midline of the body

Learning at the water tray and sand tray

A day at the seaside

Discussing Anticipating

A sandcastle with a moat

Cooperating to build a scene

Splashing water Scattering sand

Looking out for others

Ideas and equipment

Sharing

Enjoying — The feel of water at different temperatures

Splashing, swirling, mixing colours

Making firm sandcastles

Creating — 'Miniatures' of real events, e.g diggers

Appreciating — Ideas and developments

Social

Emotional

from: *Enhancing Learning through Play*, Routledge © 2012 Christine Macintyre

Intellectual

Vegetables/fruit/flowers

Recognising plants in the
garden

Sizes of plants
Speed of growth

Comparing

Providing food — making fat
balls, bird bath/table

Attracting birds and
mini-beasts to the
garden

Learning about poisonous plants
— deciduous plants

Safety in garden equipment

Safety issues

Keeping the garden tidy/
free from litter

Responsibility

Learning what fruits/veg will grow — and
what dishes they will make, e.g that chips
are cut-up potatoes!

Fruits
Vegetables

Movement (motor)

Planting

Bulbs and following
their growing cycle

Watering

Carrying a watering can

Pouring

The water gently so as
not to disturb plants

Stepping

Gently to avoid damaging
the plants

Controlling

Scattering seeds carefully

Covering

Delicate plants with fleece in the
winter

Learning in the garden area

Collecting conkers to see the prickles
(to keep the seed secure)

Collecting seeds
together in the
autumn

Preparing a patch of soil

Working together

Plants and seeds for tubs

Choosing/discussing

Taking care of a plot
together

Having responsibility
in twos or threes

Appreciating

How beautiful plants are;
How delicate plants are

Watching

The process of seeds
maturing and growing

Tending

Watering, feeding,
supporting plants

Observing

Slow growth —
delayed gratification

Social

Emotional

from: *Enhancing Learning through Play*, Routledge © 2012 Christine Macintyre

Play as Learning, Play as Practice: Intervening in Children's Play; Helping Children Who Find it Difficult to Play

Chapter overview

As this book encourages practitioners to become researchers who naturally will seek unbiased evidence, Chapter 2 begins by considering, then disputing, the thoughts of some eminent researchers who have doubted the benefits of play claimed in Chapter 1. The chapter then considers the thorny question of intervention and considers some key intervention strategies, in particular ensuring that young children learn to crawl using the cross lateral pattern. Thereafter the chapter shares decision making about intervention by using pictures as a stimulus to discern the best ways forward. Throughout the chapter different perspectives are given as food for thought and reflection.

Q: **Why do different researchers have different views on the benefits of play?**

A: Although eminent researchers and authors such as Vygotsky (1978) claimed that 'in play a child is always above his average age', and that play was 'the leading source of development in the pre-school years' – observations that helped justify play as a vitally important part of the early years curriculum – there were also sceptics who questioned whether children really learned as they played. The brilliant educationalist Piaget (1951) was one. He claimed that in play 'children mainly practise activities they already know with little modification or progress'. And more recently Meadows and Cashdan (1998) considered that children's play 'is often brief and desultory, not accounting to anything much'. Claims like these certainly gave educators pause for thought and made them focus on gathering deeper observations on children who did not appear to be progressing. For we all recognise youngsters who – in adult eyes at least – appear to fritter their time away. We all know of some children who repeat the same activity over and over again with no outward sign of improvement, and others who prefer to 'stand and stare'. But instead of imposing new things upon them, should we not be considering why? Could repetition not be giving them confidence and security in a world that is frantically busy with ever changing routines and expectations? This claim about the importance of practice is endorsed by Draper (1993) who writes, 'Practice and repetition of movement patterns result in them being absorbed into the individual's repertoire of skills, also resulting in physical changes taking place in the neurons concerned, so that the flow of impulses along a specific pathway is facilitated.' Repetition in Draper's view enhances both confidence and competence in the child and stimulates the development of myelin surrounding the pathways in the brain. This is critically important for all aspects of development (see Chapter 3).

And can we be sure that the 'standers and starers' are really learning nothing at all? Are they not just taking time to appreciate their environment or make sense of the myriad of happenings in the busy setting? Should we hurry them along and how should we do this? Or perhaps we should learn from the children and take time to contemplate a little more, take time to stand and stare? Would we not feel refreshed and invigorated by having a little time out? Perhaps then our subsequent thoughts and actions would be more understanding and appreciative of other people's perspectives and plans? After all, there's plenty of time, is there not?

Claxton (1997) endorses the idea of giving children's thoughts time to incubate. He considers that 'reflecting and mulling things over may lead to more imaginative thinking' and asks that parents and professionals allow children's ideas to come to fruition slowly and naturally. I remember a 5-year-old who asked me, 'What is *valuable* time?' He had obviously been found guilty of wasting it and he certainly quashed the notion that he should be hurried on.

Monitoring if and how children's play changed after having time to stand and stare could make a valid time sampling observation schedule. The data could, even in a small way, match or challenge earlier research findings. It would be enlightening finding out.

Activity

Observe two children who need to take time to stand and stare. Can you discover why? Can you monitor what they did afterwards and see whether the 'timeout' resulted in enhanced learning?

One alternative to watching children at play and following their plans, would be an adult-directed programme where children learn about numbers and colour in shapes. Some parents and children might prefer teaching to be more formal so that observation and assessment could be focused on specific skills. The danger is that 'just doing what they are told to do' may limit their thinking and prevent them from being imaginative and discovering things for themselves. In this mode, children learn to wait for guidance instead of planning their own way. The outcome is that children become compliant and wait to be told what to do, or 'they may even become disenchanted with learning' (Dowling 2004). This may lead to long-lasting frustration and even aggression, or the children may switch off. These states impede all aspects of learning. But of course play in a laissez-faire environment can be frustrating for children too. While some get involved in challenging activities, others need support to focus. The difference is that in a play environment, the practitioners observe and begin from where the children are.

But of course there are times when there *is* a correct way, for example to set a table or to bake a cake. So, provided the child is at the stage of wanting to learn that skill or if it would be beneficial to follow one procedure, it can be helpful to demonstrate the best way and provide the resources that are required.

When this happens, however, the result is a very different kind of activity from true play, so the balance of learning opportunities has always to be at the forefront of staff/curriculum planning. It's a question of getting the balance and the timing right for individual children. This depends on knowing them well.

Play as learning; play as practice

To try to illuminate this debate and in the knowledge that so many different types of play make discussions hard to resolve, authors (Hutt 1979; Macintyre 2001) have subdivided play into different categories as shown in the chart below.

Let's consider children's activities now and subdivide them in the same way.

Play as Learning	Play as Practice
Constructive Play Making models or building with some thought given to planning or purpose or design	*Sensori-motor Play* Exploring objects, i.e. feeling and tasting them; building a tower, pouring water from one jug to another; drawing the same picture
Explorative Play Finding the properties of new objects and discovering what they can do	*Symbolic Play* Using objects to represent live things (e.g. a yo-yo as a dog on a lead) or incomplete objects (e.g. using an empty cup to feed a doll)
Problem Solving Completing jigsaws and other puzzles; cutting and glueing to make a collage; choosing appropriate materials	*Fantasy and Sociodramatic Play* Role-playing e.g. being a spaceman or a nurse; using an object to represent something else, e.g. a cardboard box as a spaceship
Games with Rule Participating with increasing understanding of turn-taking; using a dice; knowing how to move and when to move	*Rough and Tumble Play* Pretend fighting; falling over obstacles; physically demanding play
Play on Apparatus Climbing more skilfully; jumping to land safely	*Motor Skill Play* Throwing a ball into the air and catching it (without varying the distance or speed); cutting paper (to practise using scissors)
Language Play Building rhythms and rhymes; word play	

More complex games with rules
Competitive play involving techniques and tactics, anticipation of an opponent's play and taking appropriate action

It is interesting to realise that the same activities can fit into either category depending on the intention, the attitude and aptitude of the player. A child cutting paper with scissors for the first time is learning manipulative skills and something about the properties of paper, e.g. that firm paper cuts more easily with safety scissors. This activity would go into column 1, 'Play as learning'. The child might then practise for some time just for the sake of it, until such time as the novelty wore off and a new challenge came in sight. This spell would go into column 2, 'Play as practice'. However, when different materials were available for cutting, or when the children decided to cut out different shapes, or when the children had to judge which materials were the most suitable for a particular purpose, i.e. when there was a new problem, then the activity would swing back into column 1, 'Play as learning'. Suffice to say that in most activities there are elements of new learning which need to be practised if a skilled performance is to be achieved. Most children will practise until they can achieve a level of skill that pleases them, and then, when they are ready, they move on. Playground games with balls and skipping ropes are examples of this. Suddenly games appear and as suddenly they go. No adult decrees when!

And so there are different perspectives on children's play. Some see play as the vehicle for learning while others claim that in play any new learning is incidental and that play is mainly a time for practice.

Play then:

- Is enjoyable, freely chosen by the player
- Can be abandoned without blame
- Has no preconceived outcome; the agenda can develop as play goes on
- Gives pleasure and often counteracts stress
- Develops skills that are important in non-play, i.e. work situations.

Intervention – a thorny issue. Should adults intervene? Are there times when staying back and observing is best?

'I've been intervened!'

Q: If children need to learn certain skills, if they are trying to do something but making little headway or if we know there is a good reason for doing it a certain way, then we should show them, should we not?

A: You are raising the complex issue of when best to intervene and, yes, there are times when children's frustration can set in through struggling and knowing that adults know a better way. However, a cry that has always stayed with me came from Cohen (1987). He furiously challenged intervention in play, writing 'When I hear that in play children ought to learn things, to share and take turns and be polite, I ask "Are there social engineers on the swings?"'

Q: Can you give an example of a skill where practitioners should intervene to teach the correct way?

A: A key skill that all children should learn is crawling using the cross lateral pattern.

NB The skill of crawling is so important that Appendix 3 will give extra information and list strategies to encourage children to adopt the correct cross lateral pattern.

Crawling is such an exciting activity because it allows children to explore their environment and become a little more independent. The achievement shows adults that maturation is on track – or it does if the correct cross lateral pattern is used. But if children bum shuffle or crawl using a homolateral pattern, adults should intervene and help them learn the correct way. They should teach them to crawl because this gives the brain a second chance to inhibit the asymmetric tonic neck reflex (ATNR) which is likely to have been retained when children find the cross lateral pattern difficult. It is impossible to crawl with a fluent cross lateral pattern if this reflex persists (Goddard Blythe 2008). If another pattern is adopted, the hand–eye coordination that develops from crawling suffers, and the myelination of the particular neurons in the brain is affected too. Sometimes children don't crawl at all and their parents think they have done well to miss a step and go straight to walking. And this may be the case, but many who didn't crawl, couldn't crawl. They could not achieve the cross lateral pattern, and as this could have implications for later writing and other skills that require crossing the midline of the body, such as buttoning up coats, it needs to be checked.

Let's observe Rachel first and find what learning she has gained from being able to crawl. Crawling is a locomotor skill that gives her a measure of independence, allowing her, perhaps for the first time, to go beyond previous limits, so her opportunities for playing and problem solving – e.g. will my toy be upstairs and can I get there? – are increased. She can visualise a task and set out to investigate. This in itself is challenging and exciting for her.

Q: What pointers should parents and professionals observe?

A: The picture shows that Rachel is able to hold a strong table position. She has a flat back and her arms and legs are supporting her well. She is able to look around and maintain this position. When children cannot sustain this position, it may simply mean that they have not yet developed the muscular strength to support the action. As this may be down to maturation of the cerebellum, the part of the brain helping muscle tone, it is wise to wait and try this again a bit later. However, if difficulty with the cross lateral pattern continues beyond 18 months or so, it may be that the child has retained a primitive reflex that should have been washed away.

Q: What does the cross lateral pattern involve?

A: If you look at Jack in the picture, he has one hand forward then the opposite leg. This is the cross lateral pattern. Sometimes it is easier to observe this in a climbing action or in a child crawling up stairs because then the action is slowed down. How could Jack have mastered this challenge if he wasn't able to use the cross lateral pattern? I shouldn't think he'd even want to try.

NB Adults, please get down and try to crawl. It can be confusing but trying it out means that you will be sure to teach children the correct way. It's harder than it looks! Identify anyone who uses the homolateral pattern, i.e. the arm and leg on the same side going forward, and ask them if they found writing difficult.

Q: I have vaguely heard of a link between crawling using the cross lateral pattern and reading and writing skills. Could you explain?

A: At first it seems strange to link crawling to reading and writing. The link was first discovered by studying many, many children with unexplained learning difficulties and, when their babyhood histories were explored, discovering that they had not crawled. Some had bum shuffled, some had crawled homolaterally, and others had missed out crawling altogether and simply got up to walk. Despite their being intelligent children, many had a surprising dip in the motor aspect of their development, a dip that most commonly affected their reading and writing skills and other activities of daily living that necessitated crossing the midline of the body, e.g. using a knife and fork, cleaning teeth and doing up buttons and zips. Some children with dyslexia and dyspraxia come into this group, while others did crawl on reflection most parents said they did not notice how.

Crawling and writing

Some time ago when the BBC film *Baby, It's You* was made, the commentator announced that achieving the cross lateral pattern set up a template in the mind that eased later learning. Goddard (1996) confirms this. She explains, 'Continuous brain development is facilitated through these crawling sequences which lay down efficient neural pathways.'

She also confirms that if the primitive reflex, the ATNR, is retained, a smooth continuous writing action is difficult to achieve. This is because when the child turns their head to follow a script, the arm on that side is primed to reach out while the arm on the other side tries to curl in towards the body. In addition there will be difficulty crossing the midline and manipulating objects like a pen or pencil.

Crawling and visual acuity

One of the less well known theories is that there is a link between crawling and visual acuity. Peter Blythe claims that this is because crawling helps the eyes to cross the midline as, during the action, they follow one hand then the other. This is essential for reading a line of print without losing the place at the midline. Also in crawling, the eyes are focusing at the same distance as they will need to do in later reading and writing tasks. So crawling also develops near-point vision.

Summary of learning gains arising from crawling as part of play

These pointers can also be used to form observation and assessment charts.
Crawling using the cross lateral action:

- Helps children sustain the table (strong flat back) position and develops strength in the arms, legs, trunk and neck. This enables more challenging activities to be mastered (motor gains)
- Allows locomotion and independence (motor/emotional/social gains)
- Develops balance – the practising child can topple over without being hurt (motor/intellectual gains) and so is not prevented from trying again
- Helps develop visual acuity (intellectual/sensory gains)
- Facilitates reading and writing later on (motor/intellectual/emotional gains)
- Enhances planning, sequencing and organising (intellectual/motor/social/emotional gains)
- Develops hand–eye and whole body coordination (motor gains)
- Helps develop hand–eye coordination.

It has to be said that if babies find bum shuffling or seal-like actions on wooden floors or homolateral crawling effective it can be hard to persuade them to change, but persevering through playing crawling games and providing climbing opportunities may result in significant intellectual gains.

The motor or movement aspect of development should be emphasised in the early years because, as Piaget (1969) explained, 'Movement is a child's first language.' The children expressing themselves through movement give adults vital opportunities for meaningful observation and assessment. This can happen even before the children can talk.

To intervene or not – that is the question

Q: I can see that observing children and making decisions about intervention is difficult. Perhaps observing and intervening in crawling and other skills where there is a correct, efficient way is easier. But what about times when we don't really understand what the children are doing or thinking and we don't know what to say?

Activity

In the following case studies, think of what you would do. Can you pinpoint any issues for discussion? Did Nuala and David get it right, or what other things would you have done?

Case study

Nuala had two very bright 4-year-old children in her setting. Before they arrived they could both read fluently, and they were meticulous in completing their chosen pieces of work, as can be seen in the picture. She wondered how she could involve them in more fantasy play. They seemed to enjoy stories and dancing but their craftwork was quite formal and they avoided role-play altogether. What should she do?

Nuala decided that as the girls put their painting aprons on with no fuss, they might like to take on the role of a nurse instead, and so, adjacent to a newly set up hospital corner, she hung up two Red Cross uniforms and suggested the children might like to become nurses. The uniforms were donned but the girls hung back and watched while the other children used the stethoscopes and happily gave 'injections'. The girls explained that they had never been to hospital and so didn't understand what to do. Nuala's entreaty to watch the others and learn was cut short when one of the girls explained, 'I wouldn't work in a hospital by choice but if I had to, I'd only be a consultant, never a nurse.' So that strategy didn't work. What would you do?

Q: So, often you just have to have a go and then try to work out why it was the wrong move?

A: Yes, making decisions about intervention is tricky and tantalising, but practitioners have to try.

Activity

Here is an opportunity to observe Harry, who is nearly 5. What would you do or say? Record your ideas here and compare them with someone else who is interested in exploring children's thoughts.

Harry is seeing much more than two stones?

Nursery teacher David decided not to intervene. He considered that since Harry was engrossed in his play, a supporting hand on his shoulder communicating reassurance was enough. But there are other alternatives. Perhaps you would encourage Harry to tell you his story about the stones, or perhaps you might put another stone on the table and gauge his reaction? Perhaps this would depend on whether you considered that Harry had come to the end of that particular episode in his play or whether he was still developing his ideas? It is so hard for adults who feel conditioned to get in there and support children to stay back, not in any uncaring way but as a considered choice to leave the development of the play with the child.

And if you wished to record Harry's play, what would you say? This brings in the vexed question of assessing in the affective domain, that is, making subjective observations about things such as enjoyment, concentration, bewilderment – things derived from feelings. Although no one, seeing the picture, could disagree with the assertion that Harry was playing happily, and possibly that had stimulated him to play longer (a time frame would give evidence of this), however it is so easy to be wrong, and to be mistaken in what had caused the smiles.

Case study

When I was teaching student teachers in Edinburgh I raised this issue with one who strongly disagreed with this whole notion. 'I'd be a poor teacher if I didn't know what my children were thinking', she asserted. I wonder if, years on, she feels the same? I shared one experience of my own that has stayed with me and still makes me squirm. I was taking a voluntary dance class for fun at the close of the day. One student stayed at the back and looked miserable and glum. Through the day I kept visualising her bored face until it got to the stage that I gently explained to her that this was a voluntary class – she didn't have to come if she wasn't enjoying the dance. 'But I love it', she exclaimed, looking amazed and horrified. I was taken aback that I had handled this so badly. That happened many years ago now but I still blush at the thought of getting it so wrong and it has made me very wary of making assessments like this.

That is why Murdoch and Macintyre (2005), after a five-year research programme into assessment, suggested that recording in the affective domain should be avoided. That is not to say that dispositions to learning are not very important – they are, but assessments about feelings often do not stand up to objective scrutiny. Perhaps it would be better to ask children to describe their own feelings and how these might affect their own thoughts about and actions towards other people? But of course this could be daunting, and adults would need to explore such possibilities sensitively, giving the children time and space to reflect in an atmosphere of calm. Professionals would need to plan their introduction based on knowing the child. 'Would you like to tell me?' is a useful opener, but one has to be prepared for a robust 'NO'.

So knowing how and when to intervene comes with experience and learning from observing someone with proven skill.

Case study

A new-to-nursery child sat weeping, loudly and uncontrollably, face to the wall. When other children tried to approach they were met by kicks and roars of rage. The teacher came and sat quite near the child, but avoided any contact. She picked a furry bear from the toy box and began to stroke it, murmuring soothing words as she did so. The child gradually began to notice and the howling changed to sobbing. When the child could hear, the teacher asked, 'Could you help me please? This little bear is frightened and upset, he would like you to stroke him too.'

All this time the teacher avoided eye contact with the child. All her attention appeared to be on the bear. This was much less threatening for the child. As he gradually approached, to see what she was doing, the teacher without speaking offered the toy to the child. He took it, went back to his original place and sat stroking the toy, but as he did so he began to look out into the nursery. His guard was down and he was beginning to want to play. The toy, which had given him a responsible job to do, became his favourite friend until he made friends with other children.

In this instance the teacher capitalised on the child's natural capacity for caring. By not talking directly to the child she was putting no pressure on him. Yet, by gently stroking the bear, she was demonstrating that she was a caring person. Later, when talking to the child was easier, she complimented him on how well he had tended the bear. She also made sure the other children knew how pleased she was and this counteracted the rather unfortunate start the child had had.

So interventions must be based on contextual knowledge and professionals must be allowed time to observe and understand the children's perspective, for there are subtle nuances in intervention. Observers may see what the children are doing but not realise they are pretending. Intervening too soon or without really understanding the tenor of the play can bring it from pretence to reality and the fantasy play is spoiled.

NB If in doubt, keep out.

But intervention has to be swift and purposeful if danger could be part of the scenario. Aggressive children have to be separated and then questions have to be asked. The table below may be helpful.

TABLE 2.1 Times to intervene

Why intervene?	To help the children who are having difficulty in playing well, i.e. happily and beneficially
	To extend the children's learning
When is the best time?	When the children themselves indicate that there is a need
How should it be done?	Gently and sensitively when you have had time to realise the kind of intervention that is best
Are there any special times?	When children are aggressive to other children or their games
	When safety rules need to be reestablished
	When children are distressed

Q: Can one intervene and still leave the children with choices?

A: Sometimes a useful ploy can be to add an extra resource to the ones the children have chosen. This would be a non-verbal intervention. Placing a digger in the sand to suggest construction, a scoop to suggest weighing or a siphon in the water tray might perk up a flagging idea and revitalise the play, but if the addition is considered inappropriate then the children can just ignore it. Another ploy is to link the activity to the daily story and suggest ideas that could be transposed to the play should the children choose to develop it.

And so, as they observe children and make complex decisions about what they should do, parents, carers and practitioners have to try to appreciate the children's perspective. Only then will they discover 'the colour of their dreams' (Dixon 2005).

Q: Is play always fun?

A: It's sad, but the answer must be 'Of course not'. Think of the children who are miserable because 'no one will let me play.' 'Not getting to play' is a heartrending state of affairs which impacts cruelly on children's self-esteem. Adult pleas to 'let him join in' have usually only temporary success, if they work at all. In response to this international problem, the American teacher and author Vivien Paley (2004) coined the phrase, 'You can't say you can't play.' This can be used as a mantra, rather than calling attention to a left-out child. Finding out whether this worked in your setting would make another interesting study topic.

For some children, playing is more of an ordeal than the activities they consider 'work'. Sometimes adults understand what is wrong because the children have recognised difficulties, such as autism, which make interacting very difficult, but very often there is no apparent (to adults, that is) reason why some children don't get to play. Adults fear that any lasting exclusion may negatively affect the children's developing self-esteem. If this happens, the children may begin to believe they are different, less valued in some way, and that the others' evaluation of them is correct.

Case study

Liam, nearly 5, a bright, smiling lad from a supportive home, was one child who didn't get to join in. After just a few sessions of trying to get to play, Liam was becoming noticeably less confident. He was taking the other children's assessment on board. 'They tell me I'm stupid', said Liam, 'maybe I am'.

Hartup (1992) understands this sad state of affairs. She explains that 'children's relationships with others both reflect and shape their understanding of themselves and their capacity to form relationships'. And as peer assessments are becoming more and more important to the children at this age, any rejection is devastating indeed.

Why had Liam had such a difficult time? He had recently moved to the district and had joined the nursery in the summer term when the favourite activity was playing outside on the large apparatus. Groups of children had already formed and there was a strong sense of ownership. Looking at Liam himself, his only apparent problem was with his motor skills. He couldn't climb as fast or jump from the climbing frame like some of the other boys. Was this why the group wouldn't let him play? Was this enough to make the child miserable? It seemed so. And yet that same group tolerated other children with severe difficulties, but these children were content to be on the periphery of the game, not trying to force entry into the dominant group as Liam was.

As a result, the group was hostile. Perhaps they didn't have the descriptive language to say what they meant and used 'stupid' as a general descriptor, but whatever the reason, this kind of name calling was unacceptable. Interestingly the same children didn't do this to children who had obvious disabilities and they were very protective of a child with Down's syndrome. It seemed that they had learned to be kind to these others, yet they ganged up against this new boy.

What were the staff to do? Removing the climbing frame was too obvious, and besides, many of the other children were enjoying it. The staff were doubtful that any verbal intervention on their part, such as asking the group to let Liam play, would be successful and they were afraid that if they tried and it didn't work, Liam's rejection would become even more obvious to some of the other children who hadn't been aware of his difficulty. Giving the child extra help so that he could learn to jump from the frame was another considered possibility, but the staff knew that Liam was not ready to attempt this, as he had not developed the coordination to ensure that this was a safe move. They were also afraid that giving him special attention might be resented and make his problem worse.

Eventually, Liam joined an indoors group at the puzzle table. By that time he was anxious to let these other children see that 'he could do it', so that he wouldn't be left out again, and as a result he was quite aggressive and took over the play. After a short time, the other children walked away. Possibly he had tried to emulate his heroes by behaving as *they* did; yet the strategy did not work. Planning ways to get to play seems to be too difficult for some children. This makes it essential that adults find ways to help.

The importance of being the same

Even in the early years, and parents say 'earlier and earlier', children want to be the same, hence the pleas for the same clothes and trainers, the same haircuts and toys. They instinctively feel that this will help them to be one of the gang. They can be right, because choosing friends at this age can depend on children's rather superficial judgements which cover concrete rather than abstract factors. But sometimes this still doesn't work and parents, having spent money they could not afford, are left devastated too.

Some fascinating research, again unpublished work by Edinburgh students searching for a topic for their dissertation, asked children of different ages to describe their friends. The researchers wished to find out if and how descriptors changed as the children grew.

Craig, aged 6, volunteered to talk about Sam, a 'special friend':

> He's a big, big fellow – huge really with big feet and he sometimes falls over and bangs into me. He has fair hair and he's good at sums and climbing trees. He has a rabbit and a dog and I wish I had one too. Sam stays in quite a wee house with a green door at the front . . .

As you can see, his comments were mainly about appearances – surface qualities rather than enduring factors.

Gemma's account of her friend was quite different. Gemma was 11:

> I'll tell you about Lynne. She's my very best friend. She gets us all organised. She's the captain of our netball team and she's really dependable at turning up and giving her best shot. The good thing is that if we lose she doesn't blame one person because we are a team. That helps if the shooters have a bad day. She's not very clever but she copes and doesn't mind too much. She giggles a lot and keeps us all cheery.

Gemma was much more concerned with attitudes and capabilities than was Craig and these reports were typical of the children's comments at each age.

In the early years, children choose friends from those who are like them; they have a strong sense of 'them' and 'us' and will jealously guard against intrusion. This is why children from different ethnic backgrounds and other groups gravitate to their own kind at this age. This is quite natural; the children are establishing the mores of their own culture. This solidarity is more evident with boys' groups, especially when they are quite newly formed – perhaps the timing of Liam's entry played an important part in his being rejected. This 'wanting to be part of a group' can even cause clever children to deliberately underachieve in school, as 'being different' means being left out. It is not difficult to see where parents' goals and children's ways diverge.

Having the same interests

The difference in playing patterns becomes obvious in these first years at school. Children are now moving beyond the boundaries of the family to find friends, so peers become very important. At age 4 or 5, cooperative play develops with children playing together for some sustained time to 'make up wee plays' (David and Christopher), 'dig tunnels and build a by-pass' (Robbie and Jack), 'do a ballet dance' (Laura and Petra). At this age the activity the children prefer to do is very important. Bee and Boyd (2005) tell us that, 'shared play interests continue to form the major basis of these early years' relationships'. And so, one way for adults to try helping children who don't get to play is to find the kind of thing they really enjoy doing and then plan how this could be introduced into the early years curriculum, or how the child could join others who also like that kind of play, or how children with similar interests could be invited home.

This sounds straightforward, but of course the child who has caused all this concern may not want to join these children. He may know exactly who he wants to play with and be willing to risk rejection rather than settle for another group of children. Liam did this. Although the staff had talked with him and his parents to find out his interests – one of which was animals – and asked him to bring in his favourite book to share with a group of children who loved animals too, this didn't work because Liam still wanted to be a part of the dominant group, i.e. the group he saw as having the popular children!

However, as this activity-based strategy very often *does* help, the planning involves:

- Finding the child's interests
- Preparing a new initiative based on that (this is so the child doesn't have the difficulty of breaking into an already established game), then
- Setting up the appropriate resources, hoping that interested children will come to play, or, if that fails,
- Inviting a group of like-minded children to join in.

But why should some children's company be sought and others' shunned?

The characteristics of popular and rejected children

Some of the characteristics which cause children to be left out are beyond their control, which seems most unfair. Physically larger but slim children and better-looking children, especially if they have sunny temperaments, tend to be the most popular. Perhaps being popular allows them to smile more? Certainly it is difficult for rejected children to smile; they are understandably sulky or aggressive or withdrawn – all factors which may mean the rejection is sustained. This is often the fate of obese children, as is name calling. These children are rejected and ridiculed and are often driven to seek comfort in eating more. Sadly, they sometimes have other negative qualities such as laziness and stupidity attributed to them even when there is no evidence to bear this out. Seeing this happen, 'fear of being fat' can cause even primary-age children to diet.

Popular children are 'non-aggressive, they explain things, they take their playmates' views into consideration; they are able to regulate their expression of strong emotions' (Pettit *et al*. 2006). In other words they can read other people's reactions and adjust their own behaviour accordingly; they have a well-developed emotional intelligence and are consistently positive. However, rejected children are often disruptive; they spoil games by being over-loud and boisterous or, in an attempt to show power, they themselves reject children who offer to play. Rejected children often see aggression as the way to solve their difficulties. This can be seen if they are involved in even a slight accident. They interpret any bump as 'meant', i.e. as a deliberate act against them, and they retaliate in a hostile way in return. This exacerbates the cycle of despair.

Another pattern that is not popular is coercive behaviour, i.e. when children use emotional expressions to gain what they want. Other children recognise this, and while they may applaud it in a popular child who uses it infrequently to gain an advantage for the group, they deride it in a less popular child who uses it to gain a personal advantage. If these children have been 'successful' at home through building a coercive attachment pattern with their parents, who perhaps want to compensate the child for not having friends at school, then the children will try this behaviour at school and be confused and distressed when it does not work. The trouble is that rejected children often find that the only group which welcomes them is made up of other rejected children, and the role model they provide may not be helpful at all.

And so children can inadvertently build barriers to friendship, and the sadness is that not getting to play at 4 often means the same at 8 and 10. But this need not persist. Children can change their ways once they are able to understand that others have needs, once they are aware of the perspectives of others and how their own behaviour impacts on their own chance of becoming an accepted member of the group. Some children, unhappily, find great difficulty in making this change.

Understanding other people's perceptions: the development of a theory of mind

At around 2 years of age, children begin to understand that other people have intentions and that their behaviour will mirror these, e.g. if a child looks longingly at a cake, the likelihood is that he will try to get it! By 3, this kind of understanding deepens – the children begin to develop theories, 'If that person believes this, he is likely to do this, or perhaps that.' They also start to realise that someone may still want something, even though they can't have it. Their understanding, however, has not deepened to the extent that they realise that other people may act on beliefs that are incorrect.

At 4 or 5, there are still aspects of other people's thinking to be grasped. The 4-year-old understands 'I know that you know', but does not appreciate that this process is reciprocal. Such understanding develops for most children around age 5 to 7. This is a critical stage in the development of genuine reciprocal friendship and shows that children are less egocentric than Piaget (1969) claimed.

If two children at different levels of understanding try to make friends and play together, it is not difficult to see how misunderstandings, which are developmental rather than intentional, arise. Most preschool children can accurately read the facial expressions for 'happy' or 'sad' but hardly any can deal with 'proud' or 'guilty'. This is complex enough for children without specific difficulties; how much harder is it for those who have real problems in this perceptual area, e.g. children on the autistic spectrum?

One piece of advice given to help these children is to immerse them in social encounters so that they have plenty of opportunity to see different modes of interaction. Only children and self-sufficient children who are content to play alone or in a very small group are more likely to have difficulty with interpretation of emotions and subsequent actions than children who have a wider social group (Lewis *et al.* 1996). The dilemma of artificially engineering sympathetic encounters against knowing that this is not reality is a difficult one to resolve. Perhaps the answer is to take it one stage at a time and above all to keep the interactions calm and stress-free.

Differences in children that make it difficult for them to play

Children with dyspraxia are one group who often find it difficult to play. They have difficulty in planning what they wish to do in a 'this then that' sequence of events. Given that this is problematic, they are even less likely to be able to interpret someone else's plans and appreciate the emotions that they could engender. This makes sustaining friendships very difficult.

Children who can't perform the movement skills which other children value, e.g. to play football or to ride a bike, also tend to get left out as their more able friends abandon them. This causes anxiety, even depression. Fine motor skills are important too. Children who can't use a knife and fork or pour juice without spilling suffer more as they get older as these skills become an essential part of socialising. Very often these children don't understand what is wrong: 'There's another party and I'm not invited again. Why not, Mum?'

Children with ADHD have similar difficulties even though the cause is different. These children are extremely restless. This prevents them from concentrating and causes disruption and annoyance to others. They have a deficit in the ability to inhibit behaviour; they must react to any stimulus. Their problem is much more severe than that of the 'normally' restless child who is often urged to sit still. When other children get angry at being disturbed, children with ADHD can't alter their behaviour to comply and resentment builds up. Sometimes naughty children will provoke them as a way of setting up a distraction in the class. Their high level of impulsivity and lack of ability to concentrate also means that they cannot participate in any sustained game.

It is not surprising to find that half of these children display excessive aggressiveness, which compounds their difficulty in making friends. This combination may well lead to bullying and delinquency or to children who are miserable and withdrawn. Drugs such as Ritalin help some children to be calmer, but their long-term effects are not known.

Children with any learning difficulty often have related social problems, which make matters worse. The trouble is that because they are individuals brought up in different environments there is no one recipe that will be guaranteed to help them all.

Parenting styles

Q: How does the family affect how the child behaves?

A: The family plays a vital role in the social development of children and this impacts on their ability to play with other children. The key characteristics of families that have positive, helpful children are:

Warmth or nurturance
Appropriately high expectations
Honest interactions
Consistent standards and rules.

Children reared in a warm, supportive atmosphere where parents work with their children and encourage their children to achieve realistic goals have a higher self-esteem. They take on new learning with confidence, sure of support and encouragement at home. Children who understand and agree with 'home rules' and know that they will stand, and that playing one parent off against the other will not be tolerated, become more competent and sure of themselves (Kurdek and Fine 1994) and also less aggressive. They also interact with their peers in a similar supportive way, taking time to listen to their problems, i.e. showing altruism just as they have received it. These competences are important in 'getting to play'.

Children who have parents who consistently use physical punishment in turn have children who are more aggressive to others (Eron *et al.* 1991). When children have many aggressive models and when these people seem to gain from it, it is no wonder that the children bring these hard and unacceptable patterns of social interaction to school. It is also no wonder that meeting a totally new way of doing things serves to confuse. The importance of teachers and nursery nurses understanding where the children are coming from is essential if their play behaviour is to be understood. Thereafter, these professionals have to judge how they may best be helped.

Supporting children as they intuitively play or as they learn to play is so demanding but so worthwhile because the confidence and competence children gain in the early years sets the tone for later learning. Practitioners must recognise that knowing when and how to intervene is a skill that can take time, for children are individuals and each one brings a different set of play and learning challenges. Chapter 3 explains why this is so; why children develop at different rates and in different ways, making enhancing their learning constantly challenging and consistently rewarding.

Understanding Learning: The Senses and the Part They Play in the Learning Process

Chapter overview

This chapter focuses on learning and shows how all aspects of learning can be stimulated through play. The seminal and current works of Howard Gardner (1983, 2007) will be analysed in relation to children's learning in the early years. Sometimes it can be difficult to see how 'educational aims' which cover all age groups can be fostered when children are small, so this chapter gives examples of children's play and explains how the aims are being met. In so doing it shows how the properties of play fulfil the current aims of education. As in Chapters 1 and 2, the text is organised around answering questions that parents and practitioners ask.

Q: How can we best prepare our children for the future? What is it that we are hoping our children will learn and be able to do?

A: I think these questions must concern every single adult who cares for children. As we look forward, we wonder which of the skills and competences, the knowledge and understandings are going to be the most relevant for our children's future. Looking back it is interesting to see how problem solving has become much more important. This happened in response to a greater understanding of how this kind of experience stimulates neurological development especially in the frontal cortex of the brain – the area often called 'the thinking part of the brain'. The emphasis moved from concentrating on rote learning (which is the best way when a quick response involving recall of factual information is required) to problem solving (the only way when solutions to unforeseen issues are required). And as no one can visualise the kind of problems that children will meet, they need certain competences which Gardner calls 'Five kinds of mind for the future'.

In 1983, Howard Gardner, rebelling against the widely held belief that only literacy and mathematics were critically important, and that 'intelligence' could be measured by passing tests, demonstrated that there were different kinds of intelligence, and that all of them were important, even equally so. The curriculum had centred on getting children through tests composed mainly of easily measurable items, with the result that the aesthetic and creative and the social and emotional elements were seen as peripheral. However, Gardner showed that there were eight kinds of intelligence. This made educationalists consider how the wider interpretation of intelligence could be encompassed, and encouraged curriculum planners to give time to subjects that allowed children with different kinds of intelligence to shine. Suddenly people were talking about the 'whole child' and realising that each child's environment played an important role in their development. They recognised that 'nature and nurture' were intertwined. This was a huge endorsement of the early years curriculum. It was a vital justification of the variety of play opportunities given to children in the early years; the recognition of and respect given to cultural differences in the settings; and the emphasis put on parents and practitioners/professionals working together to educate each child.

Gardner identified eight different kinds of intelligence and I have briefly analysed them to show how each can be stimulated for development in the early years. Carefully dated observations can give a clear picture of progress over time and it could be fascinating to monitor children's preferences and dislikes and see if and how they change.

The different kinds of intelligence are described below.

Linguistic

This is the ability to use language contextually and fluently with grammar appropriate to the age of development.

- By 3 years, children should show that they understand what is being said to them.
- They should be able to speak clearly at 3 years and have sufficient vocabulary to have their needs met.
- They should enjoy simple stories and be able to recap/role-play/remember characters from the previous day's story, and gradually – age 4–5 – be able to suggest developments/different endings to the story.
- Their speech should be contextually relevant.
- They should be able to initiate conversations and be willing to listen.
- They should hold eye contact in communications.
- They should be able to understand some non-verbal communication and respond appropriately, e.g. hand held up meaning 'stop'.

Logical/mathematical

This describes an ease and competence with numbers. Younger children will happily sing number songs or count to ten without realising what the numbers mean, but by 5:

- They should be able to make patterns with beads, gradually understanding 'bigger' and 'smaller' and size ordering.
- They should be able to follow number songs and should have a basic understanding that five buns (in the baker's shop) are more than four ('more than' is a very difficult concept up to 4 years+).
- They should be able to set a table for a snack or for a doll's tea party with the correct number of plates (showing they have understood 1:1 correspondence); they should be interested in counting games such as snakes and ladders.
- If they play games with dice or dominoes they should recognise the pattern of each number and be able to match it (4–5 years).

Musical: enjoyment of music

- They should recognise some favourite tunes.
- They should be able to clap or beat out a rhythm (this involves careful listening).
- They should be interested in different musical instruments and the sounds they make.
- They should move in an expressive way to music and enjoy singing.
- They should listen to a short piece of orchestral music, e.g. 'Carnival of the Animals', and recognise loud and soft phrases and appreciate what they mean (5 years).

Spatial

This involves an awareness of where they are in the environment around them.

- They should be able to move around the room without bumping into objects or people.
- They should understand forwards, backwards, high and low, round in a circle and sideways ('diagonally' is difficult as is 'opposite' and 'facing' but these terms can be introduced gradually to some of the older children, 4+).
- They should – increasingly – show some awareness of proportion in their drawings of people or objects.
- They should increasingly be able to gauge the distance or the direction when throwing/catching a ball.
- They should remember the way to the nearest shop or how to go home – whichever is easier.

NB The Goodenough (1972) 'Draw a Man' test is a good way to find out how children of 2½–7 years perceive spatial/body relationships. The children are asked to draw a man (this is something within every child's experience) and they are given a point for every detail they put in. It doesn't matter if arms come out of balloon-shaped bodies. If they are drawn they score a point. Similarly for hands and toes and facial details such as eyebrows and teeth. This is a highly revealing test, still used in many psychological assessments. It can be easily carried out and children's drawings can be compared over time to show progress in perception/body awareness.

Bodily kinaesthetic

This is the ability to move in a fluent, efficient way with minimal waste of energy.

- They should be able to control their limbs as they move around.
- They should be able to sit and stand still for a brief period.
- They should be aware of others in the environment and move appropriately to meet or avoid them.
- They should respect personal space.
- They should know where all their body parts are and that they can move quickly and slowly.
- They should be able to do tasks that require crossing the midline, e.g. drawing the arc of a rainbow without changing hands.
- They should be able to crawl using the cross lateral pattern.

Religious

This involves the ability to acknowledge and respect their own faith and other faiths.

- They should listen to and respect teachings about their own faith and different faiths.
- They should recognise that children in the setting have different faiths.
- They should recognise that religion plays a large part in some families and respect this.
- They should recognise different symbols of faith, as appropriate in each setting.
- They should begin to understand something of others' beliefs through teachings, e.g. about the festival of lights.

Interpersonal

This is the ability to be sensitive to the needs of others; to have well-developed altruism and empathy.

- They should understand when another child is distressed.
- They should sense when to be quiet.
- They should be pleased at being asked to help.
- They should sometimes play with the child who always gets left out.
- They should applaud a child who has done well.
- They should be prepared to wait for attention and not constantly demand it.
- They should be willing to share and take turns.

Intrapersonal

This is the ability to understand oneself. This self-knowledge is a basis or starter for understanding other people and making comparisons/assessments. It is an important part of the self-concept.

- They should be able to choose a friend.
- They should be willing to accept praise given appropriately.
- They should develop a positive sense of self.
- They should know that they are good at different things and that they need to practise others.
- They should recognise that other children have abilities and difficulties too.

Q: So what do we do if children have an uneven profile of attainment, i.e. if the children do some things well but fall behind in others?

A: Neihart (2003) advises practitioners, 'Focus on what the children can do while paying attention to the delays – but if you only pay attention to things they can't do, the children's self esteem suffers. Keep reinforcing what they can do well!' This is sound advice. It is also necessary sometimes to contrive situations where children can demonstrate these things, e.g. by giving a fearful child small responsibilities to boost his confidence; or by inviting more parents into the setting so that they can show artefacts or skills from their own culture. This allows children to empathise with the respect shown by staff to ways that might seem strange because they are different.

More recently, Gardner (2007) developed his ideas further. He spelt out 'Five kinds of mind for the future'. He named them as:

- A disciplined mind – for it is important that children can focus and achieve mastery in one or more disciplines
- One that can synthesise – sift information and select what is pertinent
- One that is creative so that children can think beyond the ordinary and mundane
- One that is respectful so that children value diversity and difference
- One that is ethical, for this lets children tell the truth.

Q: I can imagine that analysing activities in these terms would be quite challenging. Can you give an example?

A: Yes. Perhaps it will help if we listen to Amy talk about Sophie. Sophie is 4, and her nursery nurse Amy is making close observations to monitor what she is learning as she plays. Amy has been discussing Gardner's 'Five kinds of minds for the future' with her colleagues and wonders if and how considering them might affect her planning and her practice. Listen to her describe and analyse one scenario at a staff planning session.

Sophie is a child who flits from one activity to another often distracting the others. It's hard to get her to settle. When I began to observe her she was threading a random selection of beads any old how and looking out over the room to decide where she might play next. She wasn't paying much attention, so without saying anything I added some larger beads and arranged them in a two blue, two pink, pattern on the table. And as Sophie noticed this pattern emerging, she exclaimed, 'I could make a necklace for Mum.' She flushed her original threaded beads away and began again. Her initial experiment plus my non-verbal intervention had given a purpose to her play. I had to analyse this to discover what she had learned.

First of all Sophie selected the beads she wanted to use from the bead basket. This involved choosing colours and sizes to grade the beads in the necklace and matching each side. This took some time as she put the largest bead in the centre and then threaded smaller beads on from both sides and involved crossing the midline to reach for each bead in turn. She estimated the length of the string through picturing Mum's neck and I saw her looking at mine for confirmation perhaps. Then she asked, 'How will I tie this so that the beads don't come off when Mum opens it?' She had set herself a problem, tried to make some knots and resolved it when she decided to make a much longer necklace that her Mum could just slip over her head. Lots of intel-lectual/mathematical development was happening here. Perhaps she chose beads in the colours her Mum prefers? If so she is empathising with her Mum who is poorly and aiming to please her. She is stimulating her emotional development alongside her intellectual one. Her motor development has been boosted too, for threading the beads means that Sophie is practising the pincer grip, using her finger and thumb together to manipulate the bead and the string. Then she has aiming practice as she pops the thread through the hole. This should develop the competences necessary for writing and drawing, even for using a knife and fork later on, so they could be very useful observations and I think we should record her skill. And finally, when the necklace is com-plete Sophie has a real sense of achievement, and surely that is what playing and learning is about?

At that point Amy suggested that Sophie could make a box for the gift and decorate it. Sophie was torn. She noticed two friends going outside to play and wanted to join them. 'The necklace is plenty', she cried, and rushed off. However she had waited to finish it and she was being altruistic. For Sophie, that was progress.

Q: So, analysing Sophie's play using the social/motor/emotional/intel-lectual system, we find her learning opportunities have covered four areas. But what about Gardner's criteria?

A: Well the purpose of Sophie's play had kept her engrossed for more time than usual and this had led to her achieving a goal, so that might be called 'being disciplined'. And yes, she had selected from possible different beads and, by changing the type of necklace, had problem-solved a way to overcome the issue of fixing and unfixing the string. That could fulfil the second criterion. Was it creative? Marginally so – if she had persevered and made and decorated the box that would have given added fillip to this criterion. She was respecting her sick mum's interests and told the truth to Amy, so the activity had largely helped Sophie with things she needed to develop in Gardner's view.

What did Amy think? 'Well,' she said,

> I was quite nervous trying to rethink activities using this new terminology. These new criteria did make us think and enlarge our usual assessment strategy, particularly in relation to the first one, for 'discipline and mastery' weren't words we'd considered with very young children. There was also the point about encouraging, even making a child finish something when we'd always been taught that children could abandon an activity if something else more interesting came along, but Sophie did stay longer than usual and I think she was pleased she'd finished something that could be taken home as a gift. This didn't stretch to her making the box but maybe next time.

> One of the listening staff asked if these criteria were not more relevant to older children. The question about making them age-appropriate was mooted but not resolved.

Activity

Reflect on some aspect of a child's learning, such as Sophie making the gift. Could 'discipline and mastery' apply? Record your thinking (positive and negative) and, if possible, share your thoughts with others.

A critique of Gardner's work in relation to the early years could make a fascinating study.

Another practitioner was concerned about the last criterion – 'lets children tell the truth'. Jamie asked whether being creative in storytelling would be lost by staying with that idea. 'At story', he explained, 'I often ask the children, "What do you think?" or "What would *you* do?" and they give all sorts of answers. Should children be made to differentiate between imaginative responses and the truth?'

Q: Harry, a foster dad, was worried by his child's ability to lie with conviction and he was anxious to share his concerns with the staff. 'He looks us straight in the eye and has us fooled into believing his stories. We even went nextdoor to ask after our neighbour because he told us there were police cars with dogs at the door. He's only 3 and I don't suppose he understands what telling lies means, but will he become a pathological liar? How would we cope with that?'

A: Harry may be surprised and reassured to learn that 'the ability to tell fibs at two and three is the sign of a fast developing brain'. Researchers at Toronto University directed by Dr Kang Lee (2010) claim that 'children who fib, show better intellectual development because they can cover up their tracks'. Dr Lee explains that lying involves multiple brain processes such as integrating various sources of information and manipulating the data to their advantage and that this is linked to the development of regions of the brain that allow executive functioning. The team went on to calm Harry's fears about long-term lying by explaining that 50 per cent of 3-year-olds tell lies and that there is 'no link between childhood fibs and becoming cheats or fraudsters later in life'. In fact they claim that 'little liars grow up to be great leaders'.

So educationalists must still explore the ways in which children learn and know what they learn, because only then can they match and time their input in the most appropriate way. And sometimes they have to have the courage to stay back to give the children space to develop their ideas and ploys – for who knows what they may discover? Adopting any new plan takes time to evaluate its effectiveness, but if practitioners do this carefully, monitoring the highs and the lows, they will be able to justify the stance they decide to take.

The learning process

Q: I do understand that if you learn something, you know or can do something new; if that doesn't happen then no learning has taken place. But I'd like to know about the process of learning. If I understand more then I may be able to understand why some children learn easily and some have difficulties.

A: Put very simply to begin with, the learning process begins by input from the senses (gathered from environmental cues) travelling through the central nervous system to the correct parts of the brain for analysis. The brain then sends out a lightning response to the muscle groups to prompt a response. This can be shown in a simple diagram.

Sensory stimulus → Analysis/interpretation → Action → Feedback →

Competence/efficiency/easy learning depends on all parts of that chain functioning well. Goddard (1996: 120) explains, 'If movement is a child's first language, then sensation is his second. Only when motion and sensation are integrated can the higher language skills of speech, reading and writing develop fluently.'

The sensory system is part of the nervous system. The sensory receptors, which are all over our bodies, take information from the external environment through seeing, hearing, feeling, tasting and smelling (i.e. through the visual, auditory and tactile senses and those of taste and smell) and through the internal senses (i.e. the vestibular, proprioceptive and kinaesthetic senses that together make up what is often called the sixth sense). This information travels to specific centres in the sensory cortex to be analysed, then other areas of the brain become involved and the outcome is more than a simple response (an involuntary reflex), it is the result of a complex series of events. The feedback loop is important too. The first attempt should be modified by the experience of it being more or less successful; this is using feedback. Some children fail to do this and make the same 'errors' over and over again. They need more time and detailed explanations to compensate for this lack. This is an important observation if there is unexpected delay. It might be one sign of dyspraxia.

Let's explain the visual sense in relation to Sophie's activity.

Think back to Sophie selecting her beads and making a necklace for her mother. First of all she sees the beads and that visual information stimulates a rapid firing of neurons from the lens at the back of the eye where the image is inverted. And there it is converted into electrical impulses. These travel along the optic nerve and cross over (left visual field information to the right brain and right visual field information to the left brain). As the information travels through the brain, it is split into streams that go to separate centres to be processed. Some go to the visual cortex at the back of the brain and some connect with the thalamus and the higher functioning areas, bringing in emotions and memory. So Sophie seeing blue beads remembers a happy shopping day when her mother chose a blue scarf and explained that this was her favourite colour. This memory gives Sophie the motivation and altruism (she would really rather be outside) to continue working on the necklace. She is able to anticipate her mother's pleasure and even the warmth she will feel as the giver.

Within the sensory cortex (where each sense has a separate area), each area is divided into smaller parts that interpret shape, size, depth, colour and movement. Most of the cortex (with the exception of the frontal lobes) is used for sensory processing. 'Once these areas have done their job then the information goes onwards to larger cortical regions known as association areas' (Winston 2004). So the picture of a bead associates with its properties of smoothness, roundness, smallness, hardness and pinkness. It is only at this stage that the information blends to become a perception (Carter 2000: 175). And because all our brains are different and we all have had different experiences, perceptions vary from person to person. We don't see exactly the same things.

Q: So the energy alerting the receptors is called a stimulus, e.g. feeling pain, but when understanding blends with the stimulus, e.g. in recognising that the pain comes from a bad tooth and guiltily recalling a missed appointment at the dentist, that is perception. Recognising that someone is smiling is a stimulus, but knowing that they are friendly calls for perception?

A: Yes. There is a kind of intellectual layering if you like. And perception can strongly influence behaviour, e.g. if a dog is heard growling, that is sensation; perception (gleaned from previous experience) allows children to decide whether to placate or run from the animal! Information is brought in from memory stores to give the stimulus meaning.

These associations can, as just one example, extend the picture of an ambulance to visualising a visit to a hospital and recalling feelings of anxiety and helplessness as others looked after your child, to actually smelling the disinfectant and picturing the theatre. Why else does a dog get restless and jumpy when travelling near the vet's surgery? The associations trigger the memory and avoidance action is the result. Finally the limbic area of the brain brings in emotional links. Favourite pieces of music help listeners to relax, houses become homes, places of friendliness and welcome or rejection and abuse, as well as a place to shelter or, as Carter (2000) says, 'a place to hang your hat!'

Some children, especially those on the autistic spectrum, can acknowledge a stimulus without adding the meaning that would turn it into a perception. So on seeing an accident, e.g. someone falling down a cliff and the emergency services in attendance, they would report home about the lights and the vehicles but not be at all concerned by the plight of the injured person.

Q: How many senses do we have?

A: There are six and 'the sixth sense' has three component parts (the vestibular, the proprioceptive and the kinaesthetic senses). These are critically important, primarily to movement competence but, as the senses work together all of the time, they impact on all areas of learning. In fact some researchers claim that balance, coming from the vestibular sense, is the core of learning and that if children have to concentrate to hold their balance, their attention is diverted from the task at hand to the detriment of anything else they try to do.

THE SENSES	THEIR KEY ROLE	INDICATORS OF DIFFICULTIES
Vestibular	Balance	Unsteadiness; unwilling to leave the ground or take risks
Proprioceptive	Body awareness	General clumsiness
Kinaesthetic	Spatial awareness	Unable to judge distances; bumping and spilling
Visual	Seeing and tracking (functional sight)	Squinting; rubbing eyes; holding a book too near or far from the face
Auditory	Listening and hearing	Distractibility; inability to focus
Tactile	Feeling and touching	Needs firm touch or can't bear to be touched; difficulties with personal space
Taste and smell	Accept/reject food	Unwilling to try foods; upset by smells

The table above shows all the senses because they work together (sensory integration) all of the time. Let's study the well-known ones first.

The visual sense

When we see something, light from a visual stimulus is inverted as it passes through the lens. It then travels to the retina at the back of the eye and there it is turned into electrical pulses. These are carried along the optic nerve from each eye, then they cross to the opposite side at the optic chiasma. The information then passes on to the thalamus and to the visual cortex.

Assessing vision should cover much more than distance vision, which is often the main concern in a simple eye test. Children who 'pass' this test can still have difficulties tracking, i.e. following the words on a page or the writing on the board, especially if the eyes are required to cross the midline.

Visual-motor integration skills are as important as distance sight. The two eyes have to work together to focus on an image (convergence). Some children with poor convergence will see double images which confuse letter recognition; others will see the letters move on the page and may endure severe eye-strain trying to still the movement. This is Mears-Irlen syndrome, now called visual stress, and can be helped by coloured overlays or coloured lenses in spectacles. Children also benefit from being allowed to choose the colour of paper that suits them best, for different colours defeat the reflection of light. They may also find reading non-justified print easier. Barrington Stokes Publishers (based in Edinburgh) produce books like this. They are printed on cream paper and the text is not justified.

Children must also be able to adjust their focus so that they can decipher objects and print from different angles and directions. This is called accommodation. The three skills, convergence, accommodation and tracking, are all prerequisites for quick identification and reading fluently without strain.

Difficulties/observation points indicating a poor visual sense

- Rubbing eyes or partially closing them to keep out the light
- Bumping and tripping; slow to respond through checking the way is clear
- Close peering – avoidance of books.

And in older children:

- Poor reading ability due to discrimination/tracking difficulties
- Child explaining that letters jump or overlap on the page
- Distress at being asked to read
- Difficulty following written work on the board
- Handwriting sloping in different directions
- Poor letter formation.

The auditory sense

The neural pathway carrying sound splits when it leaves the ear. The larger track crosses to the other side, but the smaller one that remains means there is hearing in both sides of the brain. Both hemispheres are involved in processing sound and this means sounds are synthesised slightly differently depending on which ear receives them. Sounds are transmitted to the language-processing centre in the brain. The right ear is the more efficient – sounds heard there pass directly to the main language centre in the left hemisphere – whereas left-eared children have to pass the sound to the language subcentre and then through the corpus collosum to the left hemisphere for decoding. This slight delay may put left-eared children at a disadvantage if immediate reactions are required.

During the first three years, the child is listening and learning to tune in to sounds of his mother tongue – and thereafter it is harder to adjust to the tenor of another language. Obviously, loss of hearing significantly affects learning and every child should be tested, because bright children can copy others, hiding their own difficulty. This can pass unnoticed until more formal teaching finds it out. But many children who 'can hear' have auditory discrimination problems and these may be the basis of a recognised additional learning need, e.g. dyslexia, dyspraxia. If the child cannot hear the difference between 'p' and 'b' or 'sh' and 'th' then both reading and spelling are impaired. Even silent reading is affected because then the child listens to an inner voice. If the sounds are not clear then this process will be affected just the same as in reading aloud. Children with slight hearing loss may cover their difficulty by copying someone else. This is why it is best to have every child's hearing checked.

Hearing too much (i.e. auditory hypersensitivity) can cause as much difficulty as not hearing enough. Children bombarded by sound can have difficulty selecting what they need to hear from the variety of different noises around them. Even in a quiet classroom, some children find hearing the teacher difficult, as they cannot cut out minor rustles and squeaks.

Difficulties/observation points indicating a poor auditory sense

- Shaking head as if to clear ear passages
- Poor listening skills
- Over-sensitive to sounds – hands held over ears in even moderate noise
- Poor sense of pitch and tone
- Confusion in distinguishing letters
- Delay in responding
- Not hearing questions clearly affecting responses
- Constantly asking for things to be repeated.

One child's parents were taken aback to be told that the school was closing because the teachers were going boating. Investigation revealed that the school was closed for voting! The same child spoke 'thickly' as if mucous was clogging his throat. After he had grommets fitted, the problem was eased. It was good that the problem was investigated and solved before learning phonics was introduced.

The tactile sense

Tactility or sensitivity to touch is important in feeding, in communicating, in bonding and in generally feeling secure. Touch is one of the earliest sources of learning and touch receptors cover the whole body. They are linked to a headband in the brain, the somatosensory cortex, and it can register heat, cold, pressure, pain and body position. It makes an important contribution to the sense of balance.

Some children have a system that is over-sensitive/reactive to touch and this causes them to withdraw or be distressed by hugs – responses that most children welcome. This can make them isolated and peers can mistakenly interpret their reactions as snubs. Yet these same children can be 'touchers', seeking out sensory stimulation through contacting others even though they themselves would be distressed by such overtures.

The pain receptors can cause difficulties too. Some children are hyposensitive and may not feel pain or temperature change – they may have a huge tolerance to holding hot plates or going out-of-doors ill clad in icy winds. And the hypersensitive ones will seem to overreact about injections and visits to the dentist, but this is caused by their hypersensitivity. Some even feel pain when having their nails or hair cut and some cannot tolerate seams in socks. All kinds of problems arise from being hypo or hyper touch-sensitive.

Difficulties/observation points indicating a poor tactile sense

- Dislike of being touched, so withdrawing from contact
- May be a compulsive toucher
- Pain may not be registered appropriately, causing over- or under-reaction
- Poor temperature control
- Allergies – possibly eczema
- Dislike of contact sports/games
- If the child lacks protective control, he may not sense danger.

The senses of smell and taste

The sense of smell is the most evocative of the senses as it can stimulate memories, e.g. of a garden visited long ago or a hot summer when the milk turned sour. Unlike the other senses, sensations pass directly to the limbic system and then to the cortex. The sense of smell can also stimulate the hormones controlling appetite, temperature and sexuality. Certain smells can become associated with different situations, e.g. the smell of a hospital can conjure up memories of pain; the scent of flowers can bring to mind a happy event such as a wedding or a sad one such as a funeral. Whether we find smells nice or nasty really depends on the events we associate with them.

One year, on holiday caravanning, I was horrified to find that a farmer had dumped a load of manure in an adjoining field. En route to complain, I was met by the farmer. 'Ar,' he got in first, 'healthy, in't it?' Winston (2004: 109) explains that certain smells have the power to increase the heart rate – yes, I can see why – and he ponders whether aromatherapy might live up to its name by relieving stress. Certainly there is a market for scented candles. Is this why?

The sense of taste depends on the sense of smell – these two senses are closely linked, so it is not difficult to understand why children often refuse to accept new foods because they do not like the smell. These dislikes can last for years. Yet the smell of new baked bread is the downfall of many dieters, proving that smells can encourage eating too.

Some of the earliest learning comes through these senses, as during the sensory motor period the baby will put everything to the mouth. This most sensitive part of the body will tell about the taste and the texture of the object and whether it is hard, soft or malleable as well as whether the taste is pleasant or not.

We can discriminate only five tastes on our tongue – salt, sweet, bitter (the most sensitive taste), sour and umami, a savoury taste in foods that contain amino acids.

Difficulties/observation points indicating a poor sense of taste and smell

- Children may be very faddy about new foods and only tolerate a very restricted diet
- They may refuse to go to the bathroom because of the smell of antiseptics or even of scented soap
- They may dislike being near other people if they are wearing perfume or aftershave
- They may be upset by floor polishes or other chemical sprays.

And because they do not realise that others experience these irritations differently, they do not explain. One furious mother arrived at nursery indignant that her son said he could not go to the toilet because of the smell. The astonished staff discovered that some handwash brought in to show the pumping action to a different child, and then deposited in the toilets, was to blame. But this could have escalated. I'm sure all staff will shudder.

Appreciating the sixth sense

The vestibular sense or sense of balance

The vestibular sense, which controls balance, is at the core of functioning, because all other senses pass through the vestibular mechanism at brain-stem level. It is the first sense to be myelinated in the womb (it is active twelve weeks after conception) and through life it stays as 'leader of the sensory orchestra'. Input from all the other senses must be matched to the vestibular before their information can be processed accurately. Moreover, everything we do requires balance; static balance works to keeps us still and dynamic balance allows us to move with confidence that we will cope with rough surfaces or steep hills. Extreme sports fanatics are challenging their sense of balance while keeping their bodies on the edge, just in control.

Even in the womb the vestibular sense is important because it acts to get the baby in the head-down position ready for a vaginal birth. Many mothers who blame a breech, a C-section birth or prolonged labour for their baby's later learning/movement difficulties don't realise that the cause was not the birth itself. It may have been that the baby's vestibular sense was not working well before birth and the baby stayed in a breech or transverse position (see Macintyre 2011).

Insecure balance causes a range of difficulties so staff should check children's balance as a point of 'readiness' for further learning. Children who cannot walk along a low bench without being fearful; children who continue to write their letters back to front long after this common phase should have passed; children who cling and want to hold hands; those who avoid bikes and scooters – all need an assessment of their balance and specific support to develop it, rather than, for example, more writing practice where they can only fail.

From birth on, the vestibular sense functions to allow and control any change in posture or alignment. It helps ascertain hand and foot dominance which is important in writing and in all forms of habitual movement patterning. Not having a dominant hand or foot can cause confusion and delay in responding.

Difficulties/observation points indicating a poor vestibular sense

- A poor sense of balance – 'falling over thin air'
- Motion sickness, due to over-activity in the little hairs swirling in the liquid in the auditory canal. The sense of hearing and balance are located in the same place. This explains why too loud a noise can affect balance. Many children with dyspraxia are hypersensitive to noise. If they cover their ears, staff should observe their posture to see if their balance is affected
- Dislike of quick changes of direction (give timely warnings to allow mental preparation for what is to happen so that any change of direction is easier)
- Avoidance of funfairs or playgrounds
- Being easily disoriented (keep the environment calm and unflustered)
- Bumping and dropping things: general clumsiness
- Difficulty in staying still.

The vestibular system could be compared to having an internal compass that tells us about directions, e.g. forward, up, down, sideways, and allows the body to adapt to change in a controlled manner.

The proprioceptive and kinaesthetic senses

These two names are often used interchangeably; however, to be accurate, the kinaesthetic sense only comes into play when there is muscle contraction, i.e. when the body is moving. The proprioceptive sense works all the time, actively relaying positional information when the body is moving or at rest.

The proprioceptive sense: body awareness

Proprioceptors are nerve endings or receptors that cover the body. They are located in the hair follicles and in the eyes as well as in the skin, muscles and joints. They literally tell us where we end and the outside world begins. Receptors located in the muscles and joints tell the brain how the muscles are contracting and stretching and what joints are moving when and where. They have to work well for movement to be rhythmical and controlled.

Difficulties here lead to bumping and barging – unpopular traits that are often misunderstood.

Children with a poor proprioceptive sense often have difficulty being still – they have to keep moving so that their proprioceptors are activated, thus providing them with more secure information about where they are in space. These are the children who spend a great deal of time sharpening their pencil because they have pressed far too hard and broken the lead. Ask them to play a simple tune on the piano and watch how hard they press. Similarly, if they cannot feel their feet, they will thump along benches (so that their feet will relay positional information). They will also have difficulty curling up or keeping compact because they are not aware of the position of their body parts in relation to one another.

The kinaesthetic and proprioceptive senses are two of our internal senses. They work to tell us where we are when other cues are absent, e.g. moving in the dark with no visual cues.

Difficulties in these senses mean that children may have:

■ A low self-esteem (because of growing self-awareness and the reactions of others to their clumsiness)

■ A fear of heights

■ Poor anticipation of danger

■ Retained primitive reflexes

■ Increased tension especially in unknown environments

■ Poor visual orientation

■ Problems with auditory perception.

The kinaesthetic sense: spatial awareness

This sense is key in providing directionality, i.e. sensing where objects are in relation to the body. A child facing forward with a sound kinaesthetic sense will be able to gauge how far away and in what direction an object is, e.g. an approaching ball or even just the corner of the room.

This kind of information allows a child to judge his own size in relation to a doorway or passing through tables in the room, and lets him understand the spatial concepts, over, under, through. Similarly, this sense will prevent children misjudging heights and jumping down when it is not safe to do so. This sense of danger should kick in two weeks after the baby learns to crawl, and of course teachers must check it is working well before allowing a child to play on a climbing frame.

It is apparent then that these senses working together are vital for safety. They tell the child how to roll the body without bumping the head or hurting jutting elbows; they tell the body to stay compact in a small space, e.g. in a crowded lift/elevator, and how, when there is space, they can stretch out their arms to help them balance. And yet teachers rarely mention these senses to children, even in lessons entitled, 'The senses'.

Observable pointers could be:

- Constant movement and fidgeting (provide a beanbag to sit on and something to squeeze, so helping energise the proprioceptors)
- Poor ability to throw or kick in the right direction
- Inability to catch a ball without clutching it into the body
- Poor depth perception causing stumbling or 'falling over thin air'
- Poor sense of direction (rehearse 'where to go' ahead of the child having to do so independently)
- An over-willingness to take risks
- Urging others into danger (not recognising the consequence of actions)
- Poor body and spatial awareness (play 'Simon says' types of games (for ideas see Macintyre 2003)).

As the proprioceptive and kinaesthetic senses develop, one important gain is the acquisition of laterality, i.e. the awareness that the body has two distinct sides, right and left. Awareness of sidedness may not develop until the child is 7 or so, perhaps linking with the myelination of the axons. If you ask children to move sideways, those without this sense will turn and move forwards. Observing this development is fascinating, but you have to observe quickly because the children will copy others even if they don't have laterality themselves. Many children with dyspraxia have great difficulty knowing which hand to use and judging distances and directions is often delayed. Even adults may not have developed these senses well and this can limit their choice of occupation (imagine a policeman on point duty!) as well as causing daily frustrations with the activities of daily living.

Sensory integration

Although the senses can be studied separately, they support each other by working together. More and more with the research into dyslexia, as just one example, it is claimed that we 'read with our ears' (Peer 2002). Peer shows that an auditory difficulty in differentiating sounds (phonics) hinders both reading and spelling. And Carter (2000: 185) tells us that you do not have to have eyes to see, for video pictures have been turned into pulses that can be read, just like Braille.

A poor sense of smell inhibits the ability to discriminate different tastes. Hearing the approaching bus lets me judge the speed and allows me to get ready to get on even before I see it. However the balance needed to get on the bus smoothly without stumbling (i.e. dynamic balance) can be affected if the visual sense does not complement the vestibular one. This is why sensory integration is often called cross-modal transfer. Reactions may vary according to the type of stimulus, its intensity, its rate and its duration. Most people can only tolerate a shrill sound such as a fire alarm or an intense light for a short time without distress, and sensory deprivation has been used as a form of torture leading to insanity.

So understanding how children use the senses they have and how difficulties result is vitally important.

Activity

Stand on one leg until you wobble. As you do, count aloud to give yourself a score. Now repeat the exercise with your eyes closed and compare the scores.

Try to read a difficult text in a noisy train or bus. How long do you persevere until you abandon the book?

Have you ever passed a bread shop in the morning when you have missed breakfast? Could you taste the bread?

4

Understanding Why Children Are Different: Developmental Changes that Influence Learning and the Ability to Play

Chapter overview

This chapter focuses on development. It explains the impact and interaction of nature (i.e. what the children inherit from their parents) and nurture (how the people and resources in the children's environment respond to them and foster play/learning opportunities). Many practitioners ask if – and to what extent – what they do in their setting can compensate for 'a poor start' (which may be a health issue, a financial or social disadvantage or a lack of opportunity to play), or how they can challenge children who come into the setting with spectacular gifts. They are concerned that their part in providing 'nurture' should complement and enhance what is provided by nature. There are no easy answers to the nature/nurture debate for so much depends on each child's motivation/temperament and how the home and the setting work together to achieve similar goals.

There is no doubt, however, that understanding 'where children are coming from' helps practitioners choose strategies for interaction and activities that will support each child. Knowing how the brain develops and how problem-solving experiences promote development in the frontal cortex of the brain allows practitioners to justify giving children time to play and encouraging imaginative/fantasy play as well as skill development. These decisions, to some extent, will influence 'where they will go'.

In addition, this brief introduction to development might stimulate some to become involved in an academic study for its own sake, so that new knowledge can spill over into practice in the field.

Let's find what questions practitioners wish to ask.

Q: There are two questions I would like to ask based on observations I have made in my setting. The first is, how can two children in the same family, brought up in the same environment, be so different? I have twins in my setting. One is quiet and gentle and biddable; he is always busy playing and is an ideal child. The other is aggressive and surly. He terrorises the other children. I don't like to describe a child as nasty but he is sneaky and destructive. Yesterday he took two pieces from a favourite jigsaw and soaked them in the water tray. That ruined the whole game. If thwarted he becomes more aggressive. The second question is to ask about nature and nurture. Which is the more important? With the twins, can it be our fault that one is out of control?

A: You have raised the important issue of nature and nurture and explaining that will begin to answer your first question too.

Bee and Boyd (2005) call the nature side of development, 'the genetic blueprint that influences what children will be able to do'. This shows that what children inherit from their parents makes a huge contribution to their learning potential and how they use it. However the nurture side, i.e. what parents, carers and practitioners do, also influences development. The nurture side can do a great deal to support the nature side and to some extent it can compensate for any disadvantages that children might have inherited. This may depend on identifying learning differences early and intervening appropriately, for research has shown that early intervention is the most effective strategy (Goddard 1996; Winston 2004). Adults can also recognise and channel gifts and talents through providing challenging play opportunities for the more able children. This may best be done through fantasy play because the children, free to explore, can extend their thinking by imagining and enacting different scenarios or making up new games.

A supportive environment like this can help new connections to be made in the brain, thus enabling the children to learn more things. And if difficulties are suspected or known, parents and practitioners can revisit any learning experiences that have been missed (such as crawling – see Chapter 2) and so give the brain a second chance to build a firm foundation for later learning (Goddard 1996). So through learning about nature they are enabled to nurture.

Q: So it's difficult to say exactly what nature and nurture provide?

A: The combination of genes from the father and from the mother provides a unique genetic pattern for each child. From that moment in time the 'nature'

---

side of development would seem to be fixed, 'simply' a process of mother cells splitting into daughter cells until the baby is complete. But this is only true provided there are no accidents during the time of cell division. Accidents can actually have happened before conception or can occur as the baby is forming, and the outcome can be disabilities such as Down's syndrome. There can also be harmful substances passing from the placenta through the umbilical cord to the developing foetus. This is the nurture side impacting on the nature side. If the mother's supply of oxygen to the baby's red blood cells should be contaminated by smoking or by drug abuse, or if the filter that removes waste products from the amnion sac is not working efficiently, then the child's development may be affected. Also illnesses such as rubella contracted during the first three months of pregnancy are likely to damage the child's sight and hearing. This is a critical time – rubella caught after that time has no harmful effects.

There are 'unnatural' influences too. A mother might have a baby with the potential to be gifted but allow teratogens such as cocaine to affect its prenatal development so that the potential was destroyed. In some cases this child could have learning difficulties.

Gender differences impact on development too. A male foetus has genes that excite the production of the hormone testosterone which produces male characteristics in the child. The level is important in how 'male-like' the child will be. If a girl foetus is exposed to too much testosterone (every child has some), then she will be more likely to be male-like in her behaviour. This hormone also creates the differences in learning, e.g. the girls' earlier development of speech (the language area in the brain is myelinated later in boys), and the boys' flair with spatial tasks. Understanding this shows how inappropriate asking young boys to write is – their neurological development is not 'ready'.

This little boy is bewildered by being given an inappropriate task. He is not yet 'ready' for formal writing. His expression says it all.

Activity

Would/how would this influence your planning of play opportunities?

Can you see how playing with cars and toys that go places builds on the boys' natural understanding of spatial concepts? What else might you do to foster this?

For all those reasons, it is extremely difficult, not to say impossible, to separate the effects of nature and nurture.

Q: The genetic blueprint. How is that made and does that explain why babies in the same family are different?

A: At conception, only one of the millions of sperm the father produces travels down the fallopian tube and pierces the shell of the ovum or egg from the mother, and together these gametes or sex cells form the zygote, the largest cell in the body. In this fusion, two lots of genetic information come together. While all other cells in the body have forty-six chromosomes, the ovum and the sperm, i.e. the gametes, have only twenty-three because these come together to make up the forty-six in the zygote. Chromosomes are long strings of molecules that can be subdivided into genes and these genes are at the same place on each chromosome. This allows researchers to talk about G6 or G10 and identify the characteristics each gene carries – a fact that helps genetic screening.

In any subsequent pregnancy different gametes are involved and this explains the 'nature' differences in children from the same family. They have inherited different things. Their chemistry, their make-up, is different and this affects the way they understand and react to their environment. And while their parents and outsiders might consider the environment in which they grow up is the same, the children's perceptions based on their inherited temperamental traits make it different. In turn, these affect the children's behaviour, perhaps in the way they respond to early play experiences. If this happens, the parents' attachment behaviours can be affected too.

Activity

With a family member or close friend, reflect on a shared experience from your childhood. Ask questions such as 'What did you think of . . .?' 'What do you remember as being important/funny/horrid . . .?'

Find out how your perceptions of events differed. This highlights the importance of listening carefully to children's accounts of events.

Some time after an event in the setting, such as someone from another culture coming to share cooking or an outside event such as a visit to a farm or a fire station, find out what two children enjoyed and remembered. What were the most important things? Ask them separately so that they stay with their own account. Were their perceptions different?

'Understanding children's perceptions' would make a fascinating title for a study.

Q: I understand now that differences in siblings are there from conception. What happens after that?

A: Some time during the first twenty-four to thirty-six hours after conception, the chromosomes replicate and cell division begins. Tendrils are formed and these implant the cells into the uterine wall. This is the start of the embryonic stage. The zygote divides very rapidly and fourteen days after conception the cells that form the central nervous system can be seen as a ridge on the embryo. This forms into a long tube and the top bends over to form the brain.

Certain 'nature' characteristics are stable from the start – the colour of the child's eyes, their body build, some aspects of intelligence, their temperament, e.g. whether they will be resilient or vulnerable, outgoing or shy. There are also innate or built-in maturational patterns which will ensure that the baby learns to walk and talk and grow – in infancy we can encourage but we really do not teach these things. So, even before birth, the genetic pattern is there – and it may contain difficulties such as dyslexia, dyspraxia, autism or some of the more debilitating illnesses such as haemophilia. So right away there are different potentials that affect how readily learning can occur and what kind of teaching is best.

Q: What is the next developmental stage?

A: As the placenta and other support structures are formed, the embryo is differentiating itself into specialist groups of cells for hair and skin, sensory receptors, muscles, nerve cells and circulatory systems. By the eighth week the embryo is 1½ inches long and already has a heart and a basic circulatory system, and by twelve weeks the child's sex can be determined, eyelids and lips are there and feet have toes and hands have fingers. And for the rest of the period of gestation, the development of the systems goes on. The nervous system is one of the least well developed systems at this time; even at birth the baby is relatively helpless. But maturation is clearly at work.

The next part of the chapter will detail the changes in the developing brain that enable babies to do more things.

The brain

Q: As babies grow, their brains are maturing too. How does this happen?

A: This is a really difficult question because 'the most complex and mysterious object in the universe is the human brain' (Winston 2004). It is 'as big as a coconut, the shape of a walnut, the colour of uncooked liver and is covered in a crinkly grey skin called the cerebral cortex' (Carter 2000). This sounds fairly off-putting but the brain is responsible for survival, for thinking, for turning sounds into language and laughs, for communicating with others and listening to and understanding what they say, for developing feelings and for building relationships. It enables us to understand, to laugh and to cry. For the brain is the seat of the mind (Winston 2004).

The brain has many separate parts that are strongly linked and interdependent, working together to harmonise movement, thinking, emotion, learning and control. At birth the connections to the upper layers of the cerebral cortex are few in number; the neonate depends on the brain stem (for body regulation, i.e. heartbeat, blood pressure and rate of breathing), on the thalamus (for sensation) and on the cerebellum (for movement) for survival.

As the weeks pass, more areas of the brain are myelinated. The parietal lobe is an area that works early and so the baby learns about where things are in space, how they move, and at about 6 months begins to realise that objects and people do not disappear when they are out of sight. They now enjoy playing peek-a-boo and other simple repetitive games.

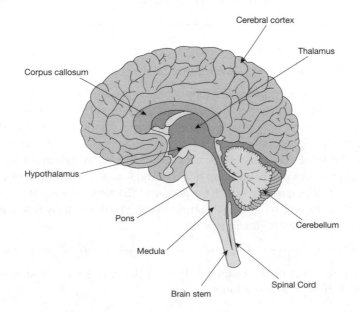

The frontal lobes begin to function at about 6 months, bringing some potential for understanding/cognition. The language areas become active at about 18 months, comprehension (Wernicke's area) maturing before the area that allows the production of speech (Broca's area). This means that babies can understand what is said to them before they can reply.

At this time too myelination creeps into the prefrontal lobes and this allows the development of self-awareness. The famous 'spot of rouge on the nose' test shows that a 2-year-old baby looking into a mirror and touching his nose recognises that the baby is not someone else, but himself. This is a play activity that pinpoints development.

Certain areas take years to mature. The reticular formation, for example, which is involved in paying attention, usually only becomes fully active at puberty, and the frontal lobes that allow control are not completely myelinated until adulthood. This explains the out-of-control behaviour that is caused by frustration in the early years. Cortisol floods the frontal lobes, rational thinking is lost and aggression takes over until calm is restored. This is why waiting until a tantrum has passed before attempting to reason with a child is the most effective strategy.

Let's look at different structures of the brain in turn.

The cerebellum

At the back of the brain is the cerebellum or little brain, so called because it is split into two parts like the cerebrum. Although it can't initiate movement on its own, it monitors all the impulses from the motor centres in the brain and from the nerve endings or proprioceptors in the muscles. It coordinates all the input from the senses and so controls every movement. Information from the vestibular sense (balance), from the eyes and from the lower limbs and trunk all passes through the cerebellum. The cerebellum is also responsible for muscle tone. If a baby is very floppy the cerebellum may be immature. The likelihood of a language centre also being there is mooted (Carter 2000) and this would explain the co-occurrence of difficulties in dyslexia and dyspraxia.

Incoming information from all the senses is vast and the cerebellum sifts out the relevant information and passes it to the correct location for analysis. There are strong links with the frontal cortex (the part of the brain that deals with problem solving). New research is finding that the cerebellum is more involved with skill development, e.g. reading, than was previously thought, but of course reading is a motor skill.

The cerebrum

The cerebrum, the part likened to a coconut in Carter's quote, has two hemispheres each split into four lobes. At the back is the occipital lobe mainly concerned with visual processing. At the side is the temporal lobe which deals with sound and comprehension (the left side only); the top houses the parietal lobe and deals with movement, orientation and some forms of recognition; and the frontal lobes are responsible for complex, executive thinking. Problem-solving opportunities would stimulate this area.

The hemispheres of the cerebrum

The two hemispheres have complementary specialist skills with a fundamental difference between them in the way they process information. The relationship between the two hemispheres is complex and they interact at many levels in completing a task. They are interdependent through the corpus collosum.

Colloquially the two hemispheres have been called 'left for literal, language and listing, right for creative thinking, visualising pictures and seeing holistically', i.e. viewing the whole picture rather than focusing on the detail, but more and more recognition of the function of the corpus collosum, which houses the nerve tracts that pass from one side of the brain to the other, means that both sides are involved together in every task.

The left hemisphere

The left hemisphere 'is calculating, communicative and capable of executing complex plans' (Carter 2000). It is dominant for language skills and for fine motor control of the fingers. Language skills cover both receptive and expressive speech, reading, writing, spelling, verbal memory and analytic reasoning. It also copes with voice information. The left side is better at analysing information so it readily identifies details (Winkley 2004).

The right hemisphere

The right hemisphere, which picks up visual cues, is dominant in social functioning, in dealing with emotions and in creative, holistic thinking. It overviews the context and so can make judgements about social interactions. It appreciates music and the arts and so it is regarded as the artistic and creative side of the brain.

The creative child (right dominant) is often considered less organised and less tidy because the plethora of solutions to a task overwhelm the organisational demands of the left hemisphere.

Working together

The brain is very complex and the continuous interaction between the two hemispheres makes it extremely difficult to work out what is happening where, but brain imaging studies show that the two hemispheres do have specific roles.

Portwood (1998) explains that if the two parts of the brain were used in isolation, and the person was asked to pick out a previously known person in a crowd, the left side would systematically search, lining up the faces one by one until it picked out the correct one. Then the face would be named. The right side would quickly scan the faces and pick out one, but would be unable to say who it was. The right side is often thought of as the practice ground for skills – the faces are then passed to the left side to be named.

In learning to read there is a time at around 7 years when there is a shift to the left side. This was Piaget's stage of conservation and it is now recognised that around this time there is a vast increase in myelination of the axons. Perhaps this is why Norwegians and many Americans begin school at 7 years. Their children are more likely to be 'ready' for more formal tasks, especially when they are based on two extra years of play.

Children with dyslexia seem to favour right hemisphere methods of teaching; they have difficulty applying left hemisphere techniques (naming, listing). MRI scans show that often the left hemisphere in dyslexic children is smaller – showing lack of development from the outset or underdevelopment from lack of use. This would be one argument for starting letter recognition early, the aim being to enhance maturation in the left hemisphere. In the Far East, where the written language is based on pictograms, dyslexia barely exists.

If the brain was split open, it would be seen that underneath the cortex lie modules and chambers, each with their own function but connected by bands of neurons. Each of the modules is duplicated in the other half, except for the pineal gland, deep within the brain. This controls the sleep/wake cycle and explains why some of us are larks while others are owls.

The corpus collosum

If the cortex and the mass of modules beneath were sliced open, the corpus collosum would appear as a thick band of fibrous tissue. It acts as a bridge between the two hemispheres of the cerebrum and transmits messages between them, ensuring that both halves, although they have special responsibilities, are involved in every action so that they almost function as one. The corpus collosum has been found to be smaller in boys and this has been mooted as one possible reason why boys feature much more than girls in the numbers of children with special needs.

The limbic system

The group of modules that lie beneath the corpus collosum make up the limbic system, which generates emotions and is closely connected to the cortex, continuously passing messages there. This system is made up of different areas, e.g. the amygdala, the hypothalamus, the hippocampus, part of the thalamus and the cingulate gyrus. They are all associated with learning, memory and emotional processing. It is involved in motivation and urges such as hunger and thirst that keep us alive. The thalamus is a relay station, directing incoming information to the correct part of the cortex for further analysis. These centres, with the cerebellum, organise the motor, sensory and autonomic systems. They are important centres for the planning and timing of actions.

Lower still, the hypothalamus with the pituitary gland helps the body adjust to different environments. The hypothalamus, situated just below the thalamus, is a synthesiser of the hormones involved in temperature control, water balance, hunger and sexual behaviour. The hormones are fed into the pituitary gland. This gland is often known as 'the leader of the endocrine orchestra' and as such controls the outflow of hormones which affect growth and behaviour. 'Too much hypothalamic stimulation with too little control from the cortex results in the obnoxious child while the reverse may mean that the child is over-controlled and inhibited' (Goddard 1996: 33). So poor behaviour regulation (as in conditions such as ADHD) may well be outside the child's voluntary control.

The hippocampus, shaped like a sea horse, is the seat of the long-term memory, and the almond-shaped amygdala is the place where fear and negative emotions are generated. These centres are part of the midbrain which forms a bridge connecting the lower centres to the cerebrum.

The reticular activating system (RAS)

Linked to the brain stem is the reticular activating system (RAS), which monitors sensory signals, causing them to stimulate or calm down the sensations in different situations. It is vital in maintaining consciousness and arousal.

The brain stem

Below that is the brain stem. It is at the top of the spinal column and is part of the central nervous system. It is formed by the nerves that run up from the body to the brain. It houses clumps of cells that cope with general alertness. The brain stem is where the nerve tracts between brain and body cross over to the other side. It controls the neurons that regulate the heartbeat, the rate of breathing, body temperature and signals to laugh, swallow or sneeze. Our existence really depends on these systems working well. Any severe injury to the core of the brain stem results in death. This is why the first action of a paramedic at the scene of an accident is to stabilise the neck.

A small number of children with Down's syndrome have cervical instability, meaning that the discs in the neck may dislodge and damage the brain stem. This is why they should not try certain activities such as forward rolls.

The cell structure

The brain has billions of neurons ('grey' thinking nerve cells) all organised into different networks that form systems that have specific jobs to do. These cells take information from the external environment, through the senses, and from the internal environment, e.g. sensations of hunger, joy and pain; they pass this information through the central nervous system, analyse it in the cerebral cortex of the brain and produce a lightning, appropriate response. These neurons or thinking cells are supported by more numerous glial cells, which, as their name suggests, 'glue' or support the network. They also store sugar as an energy source and sustain adequate levels of serotonin – the 'happy hormone' – and help in the formation of myelin. The glial cells also digest any waste matter from pruned or dying connections and so keep the strong pathways clear and efficient.

Neurons

Neurons are the brain cells that communicate with each other and enable thinking. A neuron is made up of a cell body surrounded by dendrites. The dendrites are tendrils that *receive* sensory information from receptors on their surface. The axon is the single long dendrite that transmits the information away from the cell body to

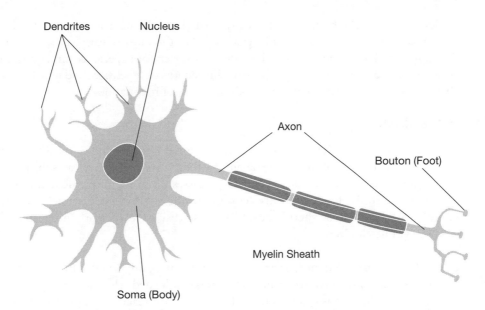

Dendrites   Nucleus

Axon

Bouton (Foot)

Myelin Sheath

Soma (Body)

This is one of many neurons, the cells that actually create brain activity. Alone it would not even have the power to twitch an eyelid, but each neuron with its branching dendrites and long tail-like axon makes a synaptic connection with up to 10,000 other neurons, meaning that it has an almost infinite number of connections. This explains the brain's huge capacity for retaining and reformulating information (Winkley 2004).

the bouton. The axons make up the white matter of the brain and they vary in length depending on the job they have to do. If the myelin sheath has built up, this communication between cells is rapid (between 2 and 20 mph) and direct.

The synapse

There is a tiny gap between the axon and the dendrite of the receiving cell. In order for the current to cross it, neurotransmitters or chemical messengers are released into the space. They carry it over the synapse to contact and excite other neurons.

Myelin

Maturation is largely down to the development of myelin, which begins at around 3 months and continues through life with critical surges at 2 years, at 6 years and again at adolescence. Myelin is formed from glial cells and, forming a 'sleeve' over the axon, it protects it, it feeds it with glucose and very importantly it eases the transmission of impulses or current from one axon to the next. The insulation provided by the covering keeps the current flowing efficiently.

In the earlier part of the chapter there was constant reference to myelination allowing more sophisticated parts of the brain to be employed. Myelin helps all the developmental milestones to be achieved at the correct time. It is critically important for balance, coordination and control. In fact part of the difficulty in muscular disabilities is caused by a poor supply of myelin. In neurotypical children we can encourage the growth of myelin by keeping them active.

Before 4 years, the brain is not fully myelinated and the neurons respond by firming up patterns of connections. This again endorses the value of early years education through play. This provides active learning in a variety of experiences in and out of doors; action songs and jingles that provide the benefits of repetition; and new learning challenges that are in tune with the children's stage of maturation.

Neurotransmitters

Neurotransmitters or chemical messengers are stored near the end of the axon at the bouton. A small electrical charge is generated by the neuron and this releases the neurotransmitter into the synapse and the message passes on to the receiving dendrites of the connecting cells. There are many neurotransmitters. Fifty have been discovered so far (Winston 2004). This short list explains those that are particularly interesting for teaching young children.

- GABA (gamma-aminobutyric acid) – this is the most important inhibiting neurotransmitter. It prevents the brain from being overloaded when too many neurons fire at once. If there is insufficient GABA, the system reacts chaotically, perhaps by fitting.

- Dopamine – this is associated with voluntary action. Children who do not have enough dopamine have difficulty initiating and sustaining controlled movements. Some genes will prevent dopamine binding to the neurons in the reward areas of the brain so those affected lack a feeling of satisfaction and are driven to seek more rewards. This explains the restlessness that drives some children and adults. A poor supply of dopamine contributes to ADHD and dyspraxia.

- Serotonin – the amount of serotonin influences the feel-good factor or mood of the child or adult and this can influence how others act towards him as well as how he tackles new learning. The level of serotonin may affect children's motivation.

- Adrenaline – this is often felt in the body as tingling of the fingers in reaction to a startle or shock; the face reddens and the blood pressure rises. This is usually associated with a state of high alertness. Adrenaline should protect the body then subside. 'Too much' explains the anxious child who appears 'on edge'.

- Noradrenalin acts in the brain to help us focus and pay attention.

So if there is a lack of any neurotransmitter, any imbalance in production, or any inefficient transmission, then learning, movement and behaviour are all affected.

Q: I've always wondered why the newborn baby is so helpless when young animals are much more in control of their bodies. Can you explain?

A: At birth, children's brains are not fully pre-programmed. The child has billions of neurons or thinking cells but the connections between them are not yet made,

---

so they do not 'fire' together. While this explains why the human baby, although far from helpless, is the least independent of primates, this status is beneficial because the brains of the newborns have flexibility and plasticity and this allows them to respond to the early experiences that influence how the brain is structured. More and more researchers are finding that the infant brain 'has an immense capacity to sort itself'. Researchers (Carter 2000; Winston 2004) even show that early bleeding in the brain may not lead to disability.

The delay in forming neural connections also means that if parent/child bonding is not immediate, relationships can still gel after the baby blues or any other 'hiccups', such as premature babies having to be kept in incubators, have passed. Attachment or bonding is a process (Robinson 2011), not a one-off event.

This process is critically important, for when bonding, a 'life long affectational relationship' (Ainsworth 1972) is formed, for then the baby learns to control strong emotional impulses in the safety of an ongoing relationship.

NB One of the best ways to nurture attachment is for parents and carers to play with their baby. This is one of the first and most important benefits of play. It encourages reciprocity and shared communication. Play like this does not need resources, only time and patience and for the adults to have the will to learn to pick up the baby's signals and respond to them.

Repetition and Hebbian learning

When two connected neurons fire together on several occasions, the cells and synapses change chemically so that when one fires there is a stronger trigger to the other. In this way useful pathways are reinforced. This process is called Hebbian learning and it explains the value of practice and, especially if the child has difficulties, the importance of over-learning. The more frequently a pattern of neural activity occurs, the stronger the pathway grows. In this way experience creates a template that facilitates repetition and retains the pattern of the action in the memory. Repetition should also promote both confidence and competence.

NB In the early years, repeated play songs and games, as well as being enjoyed and promoting a sense of community through doing things together, are helping memorising by firming up useful pathways in the brain.

The peripheral nervous system

The whole surface of the body is connected to the brain through the central nervous system with a kind of mapping. The skin, muscles and joints are covered by proprioceptors or nerve endings, which are sensory receptors (the peripheral nervous system) that pass messages to the spinal column (the central nervous system) and then to the cortex. Each finger, for example, has its own cluster of neurons on the cortex and so children who use their fingers to count or to play a musical instrument or even to act out rhymes such as 'incy wincy spider' are stimulating the cerebral cortex, the thinking part of the brain. Experiences help the brain make patterns of connections so that useful neural pathways are firmed up.

Cerebro-spinal fluid

This watery fluid made of proteins and glucose surrounds and protects the brain and spinal cord. It is derived from the bloodstream and filtered by ventricles in the brain.

Critical/sensitive learning times

The maturational process also explains why there is a critical or best time to learn certain abilities and skills. Winston (2004) gives the example of a baby born with a cataract. If this is not removed in the first months, the baby will never see because the neural pathways have not been primed to react to visual stimuli. Unused, they join others with a different function. Similarly, achievement in literacy can be impaired when children have had early functional hearing loss. If children are unable to distinguish between sounds at the correct time (e.g. p, b, d) it is likely that both speaking and later reading and spelling skills will be impaired. This is why a visual curriculum that does not depend so much on listening is best for children with hearing difficulties. Many children with Down's syndrome and some with dyslexia / dyspraxia will feature in this group but others with no recognised learning difference will be similarly impaired. This highlights the importance of functional hearing tests for all children. Over-learning and rote learning may have to substitute for intuitive learning, making progress slower and harder for both teacher and child.

So although play is the key learning activity in the early years, it can also provide assessment opportunities for discovering children's difficulties at a time when they can be most easily reduced and before the children realise they are there. Surely this is another critical piece of ammunition for practitioners to justify centring their teaching on play?

Activity

Discussion topic

How do you know when a child is ready for a different kind of activity?

Consider two very different children of the same age and list the differences that affect your decisions based on 'readiness'.

Thinking back to the twins, does the information on brain development help explain their behaviour? This will be considered further in Chapter 5.

5

Encouraging Positive
Behaviour through Play

Chapter overview

This chapter begins by considering some positive strategies to support practitioners and the children when they find it hard to settle and enjoy the play environment.

The second part explains Sutherland's (2006b) 'key relational needs of the child', then discusses the complexities of the competences that need to develop to allow children's relationships to blossom and their play to be enhanced.

Let's begin this chapter by remembering the 'other' twin in Chapter 4, the child who was disruptive and rebellious. We have all encountered children like this and know well that they are not happy. Yet it can be hard to keep positive and welcoming when the play of other children is spoiled.

Q: But how can we help? And can this be done through play?

A: This twin, let's call him Sam, has a brother, let's call him Kyle, who is a model child. Perhaps at home Sam feels inadequate and so he tries to make his mark by misbehaving at nursery? Perhaps he is less emotionally secure than his twin? Whatever the reason, Sam is causing havoc in the setting. It would be good to find out why as well as preparing strategies that might help. Not having met him or visited the setting it is difficult to know what the best strategy would be. I hope the developmental timetable explaining that Sam's control centre in his frontal cortex is not yet fully activated (see Chapter 3) has shed some light, but obviously practical suggestions for immediate action are required. These I have listed as a series of questions, hoping these cover your concerns. The answers really need to come from practitioners in the setting who know the child and his family, so forgive me if these 'solutions' sound obvious and you have already tried them.

Q: What sorts of things can we try?

A: I am sure you have spoken with the family and explained your concerns calmly without apportioning blame? This would help clarify whether Mum's absence was the cause of the trauma. On meeting the parents, begin with a positive statement, e.g. 'We are delighted that . . .', and follow that with the concern, e.g. 'In nursery, we are anxious because we want him to be happy. When he gets angry and spoils his work, we recognise that he is upset and we want to do what's best.

Always begin by praising something that Sam does, even if it's to say what a tidy child he is (even if he's only hung his coat up once), and never compare him unfavourably to his twin.

Meeting parents can be tricky because they often feel vulnerable when meeting a professional and, fearing their parenting skills will be questioned, they will assert that there is no trouble at home, when there often is. Or there may genuinely be calm at home if the boys are allowed to watch endless TV or play with computer games. Or the children may simply resent the levels of requests made at home and in the setting.

Whatever claim the parents make, accept it calmly (do not look horrified or dubious!) and ask them to chat with their son and find out if anything is upsetting him at nursery. Once the parents recognise how difficult it is for you, a professional, to get him to behave, they often open up and share their thoughts about how they manage at home. Perhaps they are aware that they give in to tantrums and feel guilty about that? Coping with two 4-year-olds is challenging and the temptation to give in for a bit of peace is one we have all faced and probably succumbed to. It's vital to set up communication possibilities with the parents even though they may be spurned (see EYPS Guidelines).

Q: Could you throw any light on why he is finding it hard to settle?

A: Some suggestions to try include:

- The top-scoring piece of advice is 'Catch him being good and give immediate praise.' This should be quietly done at first because some children resent public praise. If it goes down well, then let all the children know of the positive change.

- Stay positive. Try to welcome Sam the same way you do the other children. Avoid comments such as 'I hope you are going to be good today.' Try to convey through non-verbal communication that you expect him to behave well.

- Avoid questions where he could answer 'No', such as 'Would you like to do . . .?' Replace this with 'Time for story now. Thank you for coming quickly to the story corner.' 'Thank you for . . .' can often stop the lively ones in their tracks.

- When names are called out, e.g. 'Thank you Ann and thank you Sam', have Sam's name early so that he knows he is being included, not left last because of poor behaviour.

- Is the environment too busy? Is it possible to have a quiet space where Sam can retreat to regain a measure of calm?

- Can you simplify the environment in any way, e.g. taking down bright pictures, reducing noise by putting cord mats over wooden floors?

- Can he do large movements, e.g. painting the outside walls with water or using the bouncy ball to burn off excess energy?

Look how much energy is needed to make the ball bounce. It's also useful to read the logo on the t-shirt. Could this influence behaviour do you think?

- Is there too much noise – perhaps the staff speak loudly to make their voices carry over a large room? Children who cannot cut out visual or auditory distractors can be really distressed by flickering lights, humming noises, bright colours and sudden movement – things that are constantly there in a busy setting.

- Try to ignore minor upsets so that Sam's name is not always being called out. (It can be revealing to monitor the number of times his name *is* heard and see if there is a change in his behaviour once this has been reduced.)

- Is there something that sets him off, and, if so, can you take steps to avoid this conflict arising? Is there a certain child who annoys him? Has he got himself into the position of being the 'class clown'? It can be difficult for children to jettison this, especially when the other children expect him, even provoke him, to behave in a certain way. If there is 'an incident', monitor who else was present and find out if giving them separate activities helps.

- Can you find out if your 'rules' are at least similar to boundaries that are set at home? If they are very different, could this be causing confusion or resistance?

- Give the child some responsibility, e.g. holding the register, preparing a snack. Let him know you believe he can do well.

In a PhD study, Bryson (2000) worked with student practitioners who wished to improve their interaction skills with children in the nursery. The students had explained that when they tried to talk with the children, they resorted to using closed questions, 'just to have something to say', e.g. 'What is your name?' 'What do you like to play with?' 'Do you come to nursery very day?' or, even worse, 'What's that?' when 'what that was' was perfectly obvious to the children who were drawing! In these cases, the children's answers were monosyllabic and sometimes scornful. Very often the children just ignored the students' interventions and walked away. Bryson, an experienced nursery head practitioner herself, provided three interaction strategies for the students which she envisaged would be helpful. These were:

- To use phatics and pauses ('mmm?' 'Oh?' 'Tell me more, go on . . .'), i.e. encouraging noises or very brief inputs which do not break the flow of the children's thoughts.

- To tell the children something from their own experience which they could share, e.g. 'I remember when I was little being at the seaside . . .', or simply to wait in companionable silence until the child was ready to continue.

- Whenever possible, however, the best strategy was to let the children initiate the conversation and follow their agenda.

The students had been driven to make early interactions with the children by the unwritten and quite false supposition that because they were new practitioners, they had to justify their presence; they had to get in there and talk. Once they knew they could wait until they had observed the children at play and had something real to talk about, everyone had a much more productive and happier time.

- Can you organise the furniture in the setting so that open routes do not suggest charging around? Sometimes children can't understand being praised for running outside and restrained for trying it indoors.

- Do not have 'a naughty chair'. This only humiliates the child. It may act as a temporary deterrent but it's a negative way of dealing with a situation. It can also backfire. One child, resisting all attempts to get him involved, was asked, 'Well, what would you like to do?' He replied, 'I'd like to sit on the naughty chair. I haven't had my turn yet.' Remember children's perceptions can be very different from ours.

    Paley (2004: 72) tells of a school in Taiwan where the practitioner explained, 'I used to have a naughty chair but although the child's body was restricted, his mind entered many fantasies and his behaviour was never improved.' Asked what did work, this practitioner replied, 'Patience, and the stories of good things happening, not bad.'

- Can you ensure that a routine is established so that the child knows what comes next?

- Give warning of changes, e.g. 'In two minutes we'll be having snack. Can you begin to finish so that you are ready?'

- Could you try using a large nursery egg-timer to establish calm time?

- Can you arrange a special curriculum event around Sam's interests so that he feels that his ideas merit attention?

- Can you keeps spells of activity short, unless he thrives on complexity? Perhaps he needs more challenging activities/suggestions?

- Is there too much/not enough freedom to choose? Are the set tasks at the correct level to match his level of attainment?

- Does Kyle always have something to take home while Sam has nothing? In his own eyes this may be 'not fair' despite his having made no effort to make something. Or he may be frustrated and dissatisfied with his efforts and not know how to ask for support.

Sometimes, parents in despair will explain, 'We have tried everything and nothing will work.' Practitioners have to find ways that will. Although I am not suggesting that Sam has ADHD, in the literature on supporting children with ADHD the suggestion is made that staff redefine the ways in which they think about disruptive children.

Changes suggested by Corlett (2006) and his team (who are psychologists, not practitioners) are shown in the table below. If nothing else, this might provide some language for meeting with Sam's parents, but it is quite useful to try to think about a child in these more positive terms.

NEGATIVE FIRST THOUGHTS?	POSITIVE ALTERNATIVES
Being out of seat too much	Energetic and lively
Talking out of turn or calling out	Keen to contribute
Losing and forgetting things	Absorbed in own ideas
Distractible	High level of environmental awareness
Impatient	Goal-oriented
Daydreaming	Bored by mundane tasks, imaginative

Despite everyone's patient, best efforts, however, there are always children who challenge staff. They cannot be happy children if they are always waiting for someone to be cross. So what can be wrong?

Q: **How can we understand what is going on in the child's mind?**

A: I think it would be revealing to consider Sutherland's (2006b) work at this point. She outlines the 'key relational needs of the child' as:

- Attunement
- Validation of how the child is experiencing the event
- Containment of feelings
- Soothing or tension regulation.

These 'needs' would seem to be particularly relevant for children who are not managing to settle, who need more understanding of their plight.

Q: **But what do these terms mean?**

Attunement

The secret of gaining attunement is to understand the child's emotional intensity and to meet that by engaging with the child at an appropriate level. So if the child shows despair or rage, then the adult has to articulate their understanding of why the child feels like this and spell out their commitment to offering support. This may mean waiting till an outburst has passed but the child should be aware that the adult is waiting sympathetically, ready to respond and do what is best. It can be very difficult to know how to react, especially if the child won't share their feelings and rebuffs attempts to pacify them. The secret is to wait until calm is resumed because until then the child will not be capable of listening, far less responding. At the same time adults should try to convey support 'over the airwaves' so that the child does not feel isolated.

Validation of how the child is experiencing the event

This means trying to see events from the child's perspective and showing empathy/ understanding of what they are experiencing. In this way the adult is confirming what the child has endured. This is different from trying to distract the child or jollying them out of their unhappiness or making light of the trauma in an effort to dispel grief. Adults need to find the words to convey that they appreciate what the child is going through (even though this may be different from how they interpret the issue) and that they recognise that physical symptoms such as sore tummies are just as painful when the cause is psychological/emotional. So comments such as 'I know that was a terrible thing to have happened and I do understand why you are so upset. But remember you are safe now', may give comfort. Even though such comforts may not produce an immediate positive response, the child may retain the nuance and reflect at a calmer time later on.

Containment of feelings

This results from adults staying with/focusing on the child's intense feelings and not being diverted by outside events (which are then interpreted by the child as being more important/more worthy of attention). The adults must also stay in control of feelings of anger, which the children's distress may engender. If, for example, being bullied at school distresses the already vulnerable child, the adult has to stay calm and focused while trying to prepare a plan of action that is acceptable to the child. Overly expressed anger/dismay, even when this is supporting the child, does not foster containment. Comments such as, 'Right, I'll get in there and sort this out' or 'Well, bullies are there all the time – it's just a fact of life', can make things worse. Listening and/or waiting, then calmly discussing what happened is a good first step. Perhaps even explaining the process of what you are attempting to do, e.g. 'Let's wait a bit together and then we'll talk things over', might lead to any action being a shared endeavour, with the child left feeling 'in charge'.

Allied to this is the setting of boundaries. If children overstep the mark, then explanations and joint discussions should precede any 'punishment' such as limiting time at a favourite activity. At home children may not have had boundaries or they may have been so erratic that they give no sense of security, and then 'doing right' and 'doing wrong' become confused. Sutherland (2006a) describes these children as being 'limit deprived'.

Soothing or tension regulation

To try to support the children through their intense feelings of stress/worthlessness/ anomie, adults need to use a calm constant approach, using touch to comfort if this is acceptable. A note of caution is necessary here. Looked after children, who need a hug more than most, may see such an approach as a prelude to abuse and so adults must always ask the child if a cuddle would help and stay calm if it is rejected or if the suggestion brings on screams. Another recommendation is 'holding eye contact', but again this can be difficult for children who find it difficult to read responses or who find proximity threatening. The aim is that the children will learn to self-regulate their emotions rather than becoming aggressive or harming themselves – both signs of deep despair.

Q: If children constantly have outbursts, what then? What is going on and are there likely to be long-lasting effects?

A: These children must be under tremendous stress and Winston (2004: 448) explains, 'Stress is perhaps the most classic and common example of the way a state of mind can affect the body.' He also points out that the ability to handle stress is vital because, left unchecked or continuing for a time, it can be linked to many illnesses. This is because substances such as cortisol can affect the body's ability to fight infection. It is helpful in the short term as it helps the body react to a stimulus – it helps energy to be mobilised – but long term it causes tiredness and even depression. This is because it blocks GABA (the emotional chemical that calms – see Chapter 4) and so prevents the stressed person being able to self-calm. Aggression can result. This is because cortisol floods the frontal cortex of the brain thus knocking out reasoning and problem solving.

Children raised with a 'gentle touch' approach will produce increased amounts of serotonin – the happy hormone – resulting in lower levels of aggression. This will enable them to be positive and more resilient in meeting new people and confronting new experiences. And when they have lower levels of stress they are likely to be healthier.

So sustaining a gentle approach with calmly stated boundaries has particular benefits for out-of-sorts children. We often take it for granted that when the child is physically strong his social and emotional development is stable too, but that might not be the case.

Robinson (2011) explains:

Adults have to recognise that the child has an immature brain with regulatory pathways which still need to be supported in order to be established. This process does not happen by default. Sometimes it is hard for adults to realise just how long this whole process takes, and it is often not until the child is over 5 that they are able to really think about what options they might have. However, the foundations for such skills are laid in the preschool years and the opportunities for children's independence, learning about boundaries and understanding the minds of others lie not only in their day to day relationships with adults and peers but also in their opportunities for play. The particular element of play (to foster such gains) is fantasy and role play.

So Robinson is endorsing the value of fantasy play as a medium for developing self-regulation. Fantasy play allows children to decentre in a safe environment – they can take on the role of someone or something else and act out that person's demeanour. In so doing they learn that others have different views from themselves; that there are different responsibilities to be fulfilled; and that solving problems can be achieved through discussion, not aggression. They also learn how to behave if someone else is hurt or needy and we hope they learn to trust – but this is a developmental trait that can be delayed.

The development of emotional intelligence

Q: How do children learn to understand their own emotions and those of the people around them? When they are hurt or angry or afraid, do these emotions affect their behaviour as well as their feelings? How early can children appreciate that other people may have different feelings from themselves and how to recognise and adjust their reactions and responses when they meet? And do these responses change in any qualitative way as the children mature?

A: These are important questions for everyone who wishes to understand children's emotional development, because apart from its own intrinsic importance, it also impinges either positively or negatively on all other aspects of development.

There are many questions still to be answered in the field of emotional development, e.g. exactly how emotional trauma affects concentration and the ability to learn, or how in settings practitioners can best help children who are ill at ease, stressed or even abused. Barnardos (2002) is adamant that practitioners should know more about the traumas many 'looked after children' have suffered so that they understand the children's very different emotional responses in activities such as role-play.

Q: How does this understanding of others begin?

Interpreting facial expressions

Perhaps the most obvious answer to the question of how children learn to appreciate other people's feelings is through interpreting facial expressions. When does this begin? Does it have to be learned? Darwin said no. He claimed that all children, almost from birth, had an innate understanding of facial expressions and that they could make inferences from these and react to them, i.e. they changed their own behaviour in some way in response to their perceptions that others were happy or angry or distressed. How did he know this? He illustrated his claim by describing the reactions of his son, aged 6 months, saying,

> His nurse pretended to cry, and I saw that his face instantly assumed a melancholy expression, with the corners of the mouth strongly depressed. Now this child could scarcely have seen any other child crying, and never a grown-up person cry, and I doubt whether at so early an age he could have reasoned on the subject. Therefore it seems to me that an innate feeling must have told him that the pretended crying of his nurse expressed grief; and this, through the instinct of sympathy, excited grief in him.

From this kind of observation Darwin claimed that nature, not nurture, equipped very young children to recognise expressions and understand what they meant.

Q: **What does this mean for early years practitioners?**

A: Well, knowing that children can interpret the expressions of others lets staff know that there is a sound and shared basis for explaining why certain actions fit certain situations. If a practitioner knows that a child has recognised that another child is upset, then staff and children can discuss means of helping, e.g. offering comfort or giving the child privacy to recover. At nursery, children will interpret expressions at face value – not until they are 6 or so do children recognise that others may feel one emotion inside, and yet display another on their face.

Interpreting expressions is one of the profound difficulties children on the autistic spectrum have. Unable to interpret the meaning of facial expressions and body language, their own verbal and non-verbal responses are out of context, and other children, not understanding, feel rebuffed, move away and leave them isolated.

Responding to expressions of emotions

But what about responding? It is one thing for children to understand what is going on in someone else's life, but when do they begin to respond and what kind of overtures do they make? Dunn and Kendrick (1982) asked mothers to observe and record the behaviour of their children of 2 to 4 years interacting with their younger siblings of 8 to 14 months. She found that when the younger children were distressed, most of the older children comforted their brother or sister by patting or crooning, and when they were hurt, the older ones made a positive move to intervene. However, when the older ones were unhappy, although most toddlers looked distressed, perhaps adopting a foetal curled-up position or stamping their feet or covering their eyes, they made no move to approach or offer any solace. From pieces of research like this, it was claimed that although children from a very early age understand distress in others, not until age 3 or so do they appreciate that they themselves can do something to alleviate it. In their third year, children almost without exception offered comfort to other people. This was quite a different quality of response from any that was seen in the first two years of life.

Becoming a tease

But this new ability to comfort doesn't develop alone. As it develops, children become more adept at teasing and annoying other children and adults. It is as if the two strategies come hand in hand. The important thing for practitioners to realise is that children are now aware of how they can spark off either 'good' or 'bad' behaviour in others. At 4 years, they are also able to appreciate a causal sequence, i.e. if I do this, then this is likely to follow. These children are beginning to be able to anticipate the implications of their own behaviour for other people. And so how do they react? While many children were sorry to have caused upset, some observed children remained impassive in the face of distress, while others even showed aggression. They became angry that others were upset and this made the situation worse. Observations like this cause us to ask if such aggressive children are hostile all of the time or if their attitude is context-specific. If practitioners can find out what is causing the anger and correct it, will all be well? Dunn and Kendrick (1982) found that although many children could be both sunny and hostile, there were children who 'responded to their siblings' distress with glee, and never ever moved to comfort'. How sad is that?

From this research we can gather that some children learn how to inflict hurt but never learn to sympathise. Sometimes explanations of bad behaviour, e.g. 'you mustn't bite because it is really painful', can stimulate further aggression towards the damaged child. And so no one can expect all children to develop altruism, or even, with explanation, develop caring and sympathetic ways.

Developing empathy

It is reasonable to conjecture that children differ in the extent to which they can empathise with the feelings of another child and that some simply cannot appreciate another child's distress when they themselves do not feel it. They therefore cannot appreciate the perspective of another person. Different children have different levels of emotional development just as they differ intellectually or in their movement skills. But emotional development is crucial, in that failure to develop hurts others and eventually the children themselves. Some children of course have aggressive role models and may be copying patterns of behaviour they see at home. If these children have the capacity to decentre, i.e. to understand the implications of their actions for others and realise that in the longer term their peers will resent their behaviour, then perhaps they may try to change.

The capacity to understand that someone else is happy or sad or proud of some achievement brings with it an appreciation of the underlying events that have caused that emotion.

If they appreciate someone else's emotion, do they feel it themselves? The answer could be 'yes' or 'no' depending on the type of event as well as the personality of the child. Think of watching a sad film. Children and adults weep when 'E.T.' goes home or when 'The Snowman' melts. They know it is just a story and yet the emotions overtake logic. The audience has empathised with the emotions of the characters. The film-makers portray experiences that children can relate to quite easily, and adults can remember with nostalgia and enjoyment. 'All that is required is a temporary suspension of disbelief in the fiction that has been created' (Harris 1992).

Is this what role-play in school tries to do? Is the aim to encourage a deeper understanding of other people's lives? Can children really understand what it is like to be a fireman or a nurse or is this a charade? Do they need experiences or can they imagine the characterisation in their heads? If they can't, are observers currently projecting their hopes onto what they see and being misguided by the results? This is an important question for justifying role-play in the curriculum.

Understanding pretence and fantasy

Actors, dancers and practitioners must often learn to portray emotions without feeling them themselves; otherwise life would be too stressful. Imagine the dancer in Martha Graham's 'Lamentations'. The dancer is in a shroud and expresses sadness and despair. Surely no one could give performances night after night feeling the depth of anguish that that role portrays?

Children too need to be able to separate pretence from reality. Many appear to do this quite well. They don't really believe that their doll feels pain when it is dropped or that it will feel abandoned when it is left upside down on the floor. They don't believe that they become a tree when they stretch their branches to the sky. But some children blur the boundaries. Think of the child who growls like a monster then howls with fright because the monster is too real. Think of children who know that there is no one under the bed, yet leap in and cower under the covers, afraid to check. One 12-year-old was afraid to sleep because as soon as she closed her eyes she became Anne Frank and relived all the horrors that that child endured. Her teacher, in giving graphic explanations to motivate some children, had not realised just how her input could affect those who had vivid imaginations. And so the answer is that many children can imagine events they have not experienced and can relive, to the point of exhaustion, the emotions they portray.

Some children have a switching-off mechanism that ensures they don't sustain trauma. Children have different levels of emotional tolerance, some sensitive ones knowing full well 'It's just a story', but suffering all the same, while others thrive on horror stories and want more and more!

The 4-year-old learns to portray one emotion – possibly to get attention – while actually feeling quite differently inside. As a child I can remember standing on the pavement howling not to go to nursery and at the same time thinking, 'Why am I doing this? I like nursery.' Many children do this. They arrive at nursery appearing to be inconsolable yet the minute their parent or carer leaves, they are playing happily. Meanwhile their carer worries all morning and often has to wait and peep through the window before being convinced that the child is fine. Is this a conscious move to 'punish' the carer? Or does the child just not realise the distress that has been caused?

Do children find it easier to imagine sequences of events where the characters are known or where they are unknown? Certainly in nursery there appear to be more opportunities to play at mummies and daddies than monsters – probably because of the frightening associations or because of the anticipated noise! Yet Kuczaj (1981) tells us that imagining fantasy creatures and events in their lives can be easier for children than talking about nurses or doctors, because when they do that, they have to 'unpack what they already know, rather than starting afresh with something new'.

It is indeed difficult to understand development in all its facets. However, understanding the development of emotional intelligence is as important as the other aspects of development. Perhaps its subtleties and overarching nature make it the most important one of all?

6

Understanding the Self-Concept and Nurturing the Self-Esteem

Chapter overview

This chapter explains the self-concept and its evaluative part, the self-esteem. Often the two terms are used interchangeably but they are conceptually different. The self-concept is the picture we build of ourselves as we grow. It is the product of the reactions of others towards us and how our own self-belief accepts or rejects that picture. It has been explained as a mirror or tri-dimensional image, or 'What I think of myself depends on what I think others think of me.' Positive relationships and communications with others are particularly important in the early years because that is when this internal picture is being formed, but again this is modified by the children's beliefs about whether these comments and actions are acceptable and just and by the respect in which they hold the donor. In the early years the picture fluctuates but gradually it firms up and stays with the children perhaps all of their lives.

Self-esteem is the evaluative part of that picture and it has different components, e.g. body image and ideal self, which contribute to whether the children are pleased or disappointed by what they believe themselves to be. Their assessments may not be accurate but they endure. Enhancing them is a complex process.

Let me ask a question this time. If I asked, 'What would be your key aim in working with the children in your care?', I'm pretty sure the answer would be something to do with keeping them happy and eager to learn. And if I asked, 'But how would you get your children to respond in this kind of way?', you would probably say, 'I would try to make sure each child had a positive self-esteem.' And I'm sure you would be right.

But as you reflected on this task you might be overwhelmed by the responsibility of ensuring that each child was nurtured in a way that built self-confidence as well as competence. There are many pitfalls.

Case study

Kirk is a sparkly-eyed, spiky-haired 5-year-old, new into reception class. He is fascinated by diggers and tractors and large construction work, not interests that fit readily into the school day. At nursery his assessments spoke of his good humour and energy, especially out of doors, and his popularity with the other children.

But at school Kirk's lack of concentration was prominent in his report. He was 'not interested in letters or numbers' and 'he was disrupting the class'. When he was scolded, 'he just gazed out the window, then ran off'. There was a sizeable gulf between the school's aims and the child's interests. After consultation with his mum, an individualised educational programme (IEP) was devised, but when this was reported home in the form of 'set targets', 'Not yet achieved' was written alongside each one.

His mum was furious. 'If Kirk hasn't achieved any of the targets, then surely *they* are wrong?', she said. 'Anyway it's as well he can't read for when he asked what his report had said, I just told him he'd done very well and he was to continue working hard.'

Activity

Discussion topic: Was Kirk's mum correct? In the same situation, what would you have done?

In groups, gather initial and considered reactions to this event.

Should children be told the truth if they are not meeting their targets, or should targets always be obtainable?

What do you think Kirk's reaction to 'hearing the truth' would have been?

Pope, a head teacher of a school for children with special needs, offers her advice. She claims that, 'telling children they are good at something, when being intelligent, they know they are not, far from raising their self-esteem, simply lowers it'. She explained that she was constantly amazed by children's acceptance of their difficulties provided they understood there was a programme in place to support them. Perhaps the appropriateness of the programme and the targets set is the key?

Q: So helping children build a positive self-concept is very important, but in the early years they have so much to learn. What are the critically important things? The EYPS document sets out lists of aims but, while they are all important, there are so many that describe what we try to do anyway.

A: Enhancing self-esteem must be a process of engendering trust, very like the attachment process detailed earlier, rather than a one-off event. In settings, children learn about caring for others and ways of behaving appropriately in different situations with different groups of people, e.g. when visitors arrive or they go out on trips. So they are helped to transfer this learning to cope with the events in the day and in the wider society in which they live. Many practitioners find ways for this important aspect of social and emotional development to permeate the entire curriculum, e.g. through having children share resources or cooperate in groups even before they are old enough to discuss emotive issues such as going to hospital and to participate in role-play to ease their fears of the unknown. As a result the group becomes a microcosm of a caring society. This is especially effective if practitioners explain the rationale behind their approach, e.g. 'We are taking turns because it's only fair that everyone has a shot. Please be patient and wait', rather than assuming that the children understand why it has been chosen (remember the child who was upset by never having a turn on the naughty chair, and the one who wondered, 'What is *valuable* time?', and the one who, when seeing the double locks on the nursery door, fearfully asked, 'Are there bad men trying to get in?'). These days there is so little time to explain and remember that children's perceptions are subtle and not always the same as adults'. Sensitive children may misinterpret a gentle urge to do better as evidence that they are no use at all, or children may have conflicting messages at home and at school so that they are unsure where they stand. This leads to misunderstandings and even crises in relationships between parents and staff.

But helping each child to understand every nuance and so have a positive self-esteem is not easy, for the children are individual products of a complex interaction of genetic effects (what they have inherited and how this impacts on what they can do), social and familial mores (where they live and the family practices they learn there) and personal input (what they see as important and how this affects their motivation and purpose in complying with or rejecting the learning experiences that are offered). From all of these sources the children build an internal model, i.e. a picture of what they are and what they would like to be. If practitioners are to be able to nurture the children's self-esteem, they need to understand all of this, i.e. the children, at a deep level; they need to know what has contributed to the children's self-knowledge – in common parlance, what makes each one tick.

So why is nurturing the children's self-esteem so vital to their well-being? This is because a positive self-esteem gives children confidence and enables them:

- To recognise and value the competences they have
- To build a picture of what they can strive for
- To recognise and respect the competences/learning differences others show
- To make friends with other children
- To approach new challenges positively
- To share and cooperate
- To be resilient when things go wrong, even to rise above rejection.

These are fundamental competences, which become more and more important as the children mature and become more independent. On the other hand, a low self-esteem is likely to cause the children:

- To become afraid of attempting anything new
- To become resentful that others are ahead
- To become frustrated and possibly aggressive
- To sustain inappropriate ways of interacting
- To disregard learning altogether
- To be rejected and to join other rejected children
- To be bullied or to become bullies themselves.

This scenario, which over time can escalate, must be avoided for the sake of the children themselves and all who are with them.

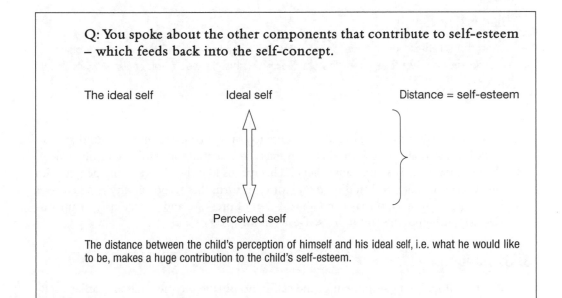

Q: You spoke about the other components that contribute to self-esteem – which feeds back into the self-concept.

The ideal self   Ideal self   Distance = self-esteem

Perceived self

The distance between the child's perception of himself and his ideal self, i.e. what he would like to be, makes a huge contribution to the child's self-esteem.

A: As children grow, they begin to make value judgements about the abilities they have and the likelihood of adding to these. If they are pleased with what they find, their self-esteem is likely to be high, but if they discover they lack the skills they would like to have, especially if they see these as unobtainable, then their self-esteem begins to wobble or crash. This would be reasonably straightforward if it was not for the fact that the children interpret reactions/situations in different ways depending on how they value the judgements of the significant others in the relationships they build, or how accurately they self-assess.

Case study

One teacher set out to investigate this issue with a group of 6-year-olds. After having fun going round an obstacle course, she asked them to think about how they had done and asked them to give themselves a mark out of 10. She was bemused that one child who had knocked hoops over instead of climbing through and who had scored no goals either at throwing or kicking awarded himself 8½. Was the child in denial? Was this his way of coping or did he genuinely believe he was much more able than was the case?

Activity

Discussion topic

What should the teacher have done? Was 'nothing' an option? Would the decision depend on how well she knew the child or how able he was in other aspects of the curriculum?

In the earliest days, secure attachments to parents or carers give a sound start to building a strong self-esteem, then at nursery and school the staff take on the role of the children's 'most significant others'. This means that they become the people with most responsibility for building the picture. In turn, this responsibility is taken over by the peer group who may exert a great deal of pressure and consciously or unconsciously influence the children's self-esteem for good or bad.

Body image

Another important component of the self-concept (the picture) that also affects self-esteem (the evaluation) is body image, and sadly even very young children can compare their body image to their ideal, find themselves wanting and take inordinate steps, e.g. dieting inappropriately, to change their shape. Glamorous images portrayed in the media endorse feelings of inadequacy and while children with a high self-esteem can recognise the artificiality of what they see, or know they are too young to look like that, or shrug off the effects of knowing they fall short of this ideal, those with a low self-esteem have their confidence knocked and negatively reinforced when efforts to change are not met with (instant) success. Again the children's perceptions may not be true. Think of those children with anorexia who believe they are fat despite evidence and reassurance to the contrary. Adults' entreaties can fall on deaf ears. The visual evidence does not counteract the usually psychological problem that diminishes their self-belief.

While this is an extreme example, children in the early years, when superficial characteristics are more important, do recognise that very often the most popular children are tall, slim and good at sports.

Does this mean that children have to be clever or slim and pretty or strongly built and muscular if they are to have a positive self-esteem? Perhaps not completely, but body image plays an important part. But again the answer is more complex that it would first appear. Children have different standards and different priorities in what they see as important. Some value academic work, others the ability to make friends, while many see movement skill as the most desirable competence. This means they have different value judgements. Whatever they are, the key to the self-esteem is the amount of discrepancy between what the child desires and what he thinks his own relative status is. Being good at something else and being praised for achievement in that area will not raise a child's self-esteem. This is why it is so important for adults to discover the things that are important to each child and do what they can to promote competence so that confidence will follow.

Very often practitioners can be surprised by the 'success' of children who have only modest intellectual qualities. Dowling (2004) points out that they may be blessed with 'emotional stamina' which allows them to have insights into the lives of others and a highly developed level of empathy. So their strengths are in building relationships with others, traits that enable them to overcome other hurdles, because 'being a good friend' is a quality highly valued by the peer group, especially beyond the nursery.

Again the issue may be clouded by children's wishes to be 'the same'. These can even override pride in the competences they wish to have. So while very clever children often outwardly deny their aptitude so that they appear to be the same as their peers, those with difficulties, unable to make any change, often despair because they see the gap between themselves and 'the desired state' as unbridgeable. To try to raise their image in the eyes of the peer group they may resort to being the class clown and be encouraged in that behaviour by others who, in the end, still reject them as friends. Alternatively they may become aggressive or withdrawn.

Yet there are many within these groups who, despite derision, have the confidence to be themselves. They stand up for the things they believe in. They refuse to change. Why can they resist the pressure? Perhaps the children's temperament is important here.

Temperamental traits

Children are born with temperamental traits – in a biological model these would be called emotional reactivates – and they are carried in the genes. This explains why personality characteristics can be resistant to change. It is interesting to note that identical twins, even those brought up separately, have marked similarities in the temperaments they display (Bee and Boyd 2005). This confirms the genetic influence on behaviour, though no researcher would deny that environment plays a part in shaping temperament too. This kind of change is learned rather than innate. It allows children to adapt to the circumstances in which they find themselves and their perceptions of what kind of behaviour they wish, or are advised, to display.

These traits – and as yet there is no agreement on the definitive group – may be placed on a continuum and they can explain why children brought up in the same environment can react so differently to what would appear to be the same events. Some examples could be:

Resilient	↔	Vulnerable
Extravert	↔	Introvert
Exuberant	↔	Passive
Impulsive	↔	Reflective
Enthusiastic	↔	Reluctant

And there are many more polar constructs. Perhaps practitioners could reflect on children they know well and devise their own?

To avoid huge lists, researchers have attempted to collate these traits into like groups. Buss and Plomin (1986) suggest only three dimensions, i.e. *emotionality, activity* and *sociability*, and these have been widely used to assess temperament in infants and young children. Similarly, Thomas and Chess (1977) have clustered their early group of nine dimensions into just three: 'The easy child, the difficult child and the slow-to-warm-up child.' I expect that practitioners will empathise with these descriptors and be able to allocate each of their children to one of these categories. The question as to whether these characteristics stay the same in different social situations is an intriguing one.

I find the first dimension in my own list particularly interesting. This concerns resilience and vulnerability. In the same situation – even in a severely disadvantaged one – the resilient child will see the positives and come up smiling. This may be because they have 'protective factors' such as a high IQ or secure attachments that buttress them against the stresses that defeat the vulnerable ones. Some children who have to be taken into care and who have had horrendous experiences can still smile. Perhaps this is a survival strategy. On the other hand, more vulnerable children tend to focus on the downsides and fail to overcome the hurts and disadvantages that accost them. In extreme cases this can lead to illness and depression. But even in everyday events at home or at school, resilient children will be able to shrug off happenings that give anguish to the vulnerable ones. The environment (families, practitioners and those in the community) must recognise and take steps to support the vulnerable ones and consistently and constantly show them that when they see something is half empty it is also half full.

How does the support children receive at home give them the confidence to be themselves? A no-win scenario arises if parents attempt to bribe their children to do better, for then the children's views of themselves as inadequate are confirmed. Alternatively, some parents, intending to offer comfort, may explain, 'You don't have to do well – we didn't.' Unfortunately the child may resent these low expectations or accept them and give up trying altogether.

Q: Can you outline the age changes? Are they fixed – or what can change them?

A: Children begin to have a sense of who they are at around 18 months, when they realise that they are separate entities and that their actions impinge on other people and gradually they become more self-aware. At this time they begin to internalise the reactions of others and form the basis of a self-concept. In the early years when all experiences are new, the children need time to judge how well they are coping and do not compare their 'performance' to anyone else, so the potential to enhance self-esteem is there. The internal model is fluctuating at this time and is responsive to being supported by positive input and chances to be successful. Gradually, however, the evaluation crystallises as a result of major events, changes in maturation and the children's perception of security at home.

Q: How can practitioners recognise children with low self-esteem?

A: Children react to feelings of inadequacy in different ways. They may be withdrawn and be very reluctant to join in; they may adopt a 'don't care because I don't want to do it anyway' approach; or very sadly they may become a bully to try to hide their feelings of inadequacy. They may prevent other children doing what they themselves cannot do, or become the class clown – a role that can be hard to drop, especially if this is the only way they see themselves as gaining attention. No matter what, they are unhappy children who need time and patience and understanding – not always easy to give if the child rejects a sympathetic but firm approach. Perseverance and not losing faith that kindness works is the only way, although it can be hard to sustain.

Although the early years period is undoubtedly the best time, it is never too late to enhance children's self-esteem. When children appear locked in to poor behaviour, perhaps making them aware of the characteristics of popular children might help them to see how their actions are causing others to see them in a negative light. In a video on 'Exclusion' the researchers asked 'excluded for violence' children to recall what they did and then they asked them, 'What do you think the others will think of you for doing that?' 'What do you think of yourself?' (This is the tri-dimensional image.) They were trying to help the children appreciate the views of other people, that is to develop their theory of mind. And at the end of the film the youngsters, who had displayed a high level of aggression towards their carers and practitioners, accepted with pride a certificate that said they had completed a ten-week course. This was the first award they had ever had. So, given self-belief, even 'hardened youngsters' can change.

NB Find new ways of being positive, e.g. I visited one class where the children were drawing self-portraits of their own face – a favourite activity in many schools. In this one, a Catholic school, the practitioner had written at the top of the page, 'God made something wonderful', and under the drawing each child wrote, 'It was ME!'

Enhancing the children's self-esteem should contribute to happier children who in turn become adults who can function well, socially, intellectually and emotionally. Can anything be more worthwhile? After all, in the words of one school's motto, 'It is to the young that the future belongs.'

7

Recording Observations: Beginning Research

Chapter overview

As carrying out a small-scale piece of research is often an important component of a further qualification, this chapter explains the basics of formalising observations, assessments and interventions, i.e. usual practices, so that the 'findings' or what has been discovered can merit the descriptor 'research'. It also considers other methods – e.g. distributing questionnaires or following up claims made in published research – which could usefully provide new thinking and information.

Any research report involves setting out clearly what is to be investigated, recording the process and drawing conclusions based on what has been discovered. All of this is governed by a set of 'rules' designed to ensure that the findings are objective, as free as possible from bias, and that claims made – perhaps claiming the benefits of a carefully planned intervention for a small group of children – can stand scrutiny by those versed in research procedures. This is vital because then the claims could legitimately be applied to other children in other settings, thus spreading the good work, allowing others to benefit from it and perhaps encouraging them either to replicate the investigation in another setting or to take the investigation further. It goes without saying that any proposed change would be to benefit the children. On the other hand, if the intervention did not produce the anticipated or hypothesised result, the investigation is not wasted, for other practitioners could share the process and the reasoning and so avoid the pitfalls in their own setting. Research need not 'work' to be successful. Success comes in setting out a careful plan, following a set of research rules, and so discovering, confronting and recording discoveries and dilemmas before drawing conclusions. This sounds a little tedious but adhering to a discipline also provides security that the correct steps in a complex undertaking are being followed. Above all, finding something new that supports your own children in your setting is fascinating, confidence-giving and so worthwhile. Becoming a researcher is true professional development.

The key starting point would be to decide, 'What is it that I want to find out?', and to phrase that in terms of the first part of a research question. Writing an answer is much harder than it sounds for it subsumes a number of considerations, e.g.

Why do I want to know this? How will the children benefit?
If I introduce a new plan, what will have to change?
How many children will I study and why have these children been chosen?

(Remember that if the number is too small (fewer than 3) then one child being absent can scupper the investigation, while a larger number means it can be difficult to observe adequately unless the idea can be used as group research. Then time is needed to discuss the process with the colleagues who are involved, but this can be a form of professional development.)

How long will this take? Making a time plan

This depends on the scope of the plan. A plan that looks at changes in children's development will obviously take much longer than studying the effects of introducing a new resource or gathering data, e.g. about parents' thoughts, so time planning has to be considered from the start.

Taking crawling as one example; an investigation might start by checking whether all the children coming into the setting could crawl using the cross lateral pattern – say by the time they are 15 months (this should be done for all age groups). The next issue would be to find the best ways to teach crawling and what games would promote it. If the research questions stopped there, i.e. only covering the incidence of children being able to crawl, the ways of teaching crawling, and sharing the activities with others, the time taken would be relatively short. But if the claims of later links with reading, writing and tracking were to be considered then the research would take at least two years. Of course the plan could happen in stages, developing as the outcomes became known.

So research can formalise what would be happening anyway, monitoring some profound change or testing some advised policy change in a particular setting for specific children. The possibilities are endless. Many new researchers wish to find 'an original topic', something that no one has studied before, and they are disappointed when they discover how difficult this is. However researching any topic in a new setting with different staff and children will produce up-to-date findings that are very worthwhile.

Moreover any research will need an implicit time plan built in because 'improvements' need to be monitored on several occasions. Sustained changes do not happen overnight. This would be an important consideration if essays and dissertations depended on the results.

Do I need to ask permission from the parents?

Again this depends on what you wish to investigate and whether the finished work will be reported to others. Having said that, it is always best to get written permission so that there are no comebacks. This is vital if the use of photos or video is anticipated.

Both audio and video recordings help objectivity and allow repeated listenings and viewings so that observations and assessments can be checked. These can also avoid lengthy explanations to parents and/or outside experts, e.g. physiotherapists can see children's poor muscle tone as they climb on apparatus, or speech and language therapists can listen to indistinct responses the children have made at story time. However these techniques can be difficult to use and very often the children, aware they are on film, change their behaviour. Of course, if they can 'do it better' because the camera is there, then this may prevent further worries. Another ploy is to have the camera in the setting recording everyday events until the children ignore it – and then film.

Confidentiality

Researchers have to reassure the parents that in any recording or discussion beyond the setting, children's names will be changed and (only if this is possible) faces will be blurred to prevent recognition. Even if the families say this is unnecessary it is best to err on the safe side in case the family circumstances change and recognising the child becomes a problem. However remote the possibility, it is best to be safe, and this also shows you have followed the rules of research. What you have done should be documented in writing up the research procedures.

NB File and keep the signed letters safe because parents can forget they gave permission.

Sample letter

Dear (parent's name),

As part of my study for EYPS, I aim to carry out a small piece of research with a group of chosen children and I would like your permission to have (child's name) in this group. The purpose of the study is to find out how gender differences in children affect their learning so the group has three boys and three girls. I would be monitoring what play choices children make, if there are differences between girls' choices and those made by boys and how skilled they are at what they choose to do. This is to help staff discover what the best kind of activities might be. The findings might lead to some curriculum changes next year but these will not affect these 4-year-olds who will have moved into Reception class.

(Child's name) will be unaware that this study – which is to make our support more effective – is taking place and I ask that you don't discuss this with him. I am anxious not to change the children's behaviour in any way or to make them anxious.

The tear-off slip below asks you (1) to sign if you agree to (child's name) taking part and (2) to sign again if you agree to video being used to capture episodes of the children at play. These would be used for educational purposes only and any findings could be shared with you if you would like that. If you do not wish your child to participate, please say. That is perfectly alright.

Please return this form in the enclosed envelope by Friday (date).

Using questionnaires

This is a different kind of research which sets out to find the views of a larger group of people rather than observing a few children closely and monitoring the effects of the change on their behaviour/learning.

Again this type of research is difficult. It is not easy to set unambiguous questions because the recipients don't always interpret questions in the anticipated way. It can be only too easy to gather data then find the questions you asked or the schedules you have devised do not illuminate the points you wanted to explore. I have had many students wail, 'What did they tell me that for?', and the only answer was, 'Because that is the answer to the questions you asked.' Sadly the rejoinder, 'But I didn't mean that at all', doesn't resolve the issue!

Key advice: always do a small-scale pilot study with people you know, so that they will reply 'honestly' and if they do not understand what you mean they will tell you so in time for you to make the items clearer. If you have asked questions and your pilot group produces surprising replies, this also points to misunderstandings. So carefully examine the answers in relation to the questions before you actually distribute the final version. Almost inevitably your questions will need to be reformulated. This is vital. Be prepared to take time to clarify what it is you want to discover.

The timing of giving out the questionnaires and the method of collecting the replies have also to be worked out in the light of respecting confidentiality. If this is not observed – if for example the parents have to hand you a completed questionnaire instead of putting it in an out-of-sight box with others – then bias will likely result, for anxious-to-please parents will tell you what they think you want to know and defeat the whole purpose of the research.

Reducing bias in the collection of data

NB Bias is really distortion or skewed recordings because not enough preliminary steps have been taken, e.g. taking a random selection of children for study rather then selecting those who will be biddable. It is impossible to eradicate all bias but researchers have to be seen to take steps to reduce it.

Moves to reduce bias are vitally important for objectivity. One way is to have different staff record their observations and to compare the findings. This is sound research because it means that more than one pair of eyes, and so different perceptions of events, are involved. Different recorders can also prevent the children feeling they are being scrutinised and changing their usual behaviour. Another way to reduce bias is to review the claimed improvement in different situations, e.g. if you have encouraged boys and girls to play together indoors (to try to reduce gender bias in the selection of activities and so extend the skill base of both boys and girls), does this transfer to their playing together out of doors or in forming friendships? Do these spontaneous friendship groupings endure? In any research report, all these considerations would have to be detailed.

Following up 'someone else's claims' in your setting

This type of research can be equally fascinating and thought-provoking. For example, in Chapter 3 (p. 65), parents were mollified by the claim that 'the ability to tell fibs at two and three is the sign of a fast developing brain'.

> Researchers at Toronto University directed by Dr Kang Lee (2010) claim that 'children who fib, show better intellectual development because they can cover up their tracks'. Dr Lee explains that lying involves multiple brain processes such as integrating various sources of information and manipulating the data to their advantage and that this is linked to the development of regions of the brain that allow executive functioning.

A useful piece of research might be to find out how 'telling lies' is received/perpetuated/refuted by staff and to consider in the light of Lee's findings what should be done.

There is a dilemma in that favourite stories are based on 'lies' – e.g. the three bears don't really live in a house in the forest – as are the tooth fairy and Santa. And yet 'developing creativity' is a key educational aim. The question as to whether children's imagination/education would be limited by outlawing fantasy – and how this would be done in the setting – could be a novel and fascinating starting point.

Play provides many such opportunities for research. Do Piaget's changes still apply? Does Vygotsky's claim about the stage of proximal development hold true? What are babies really learning when they play with treasure baskets? And what are young children conveying through movement even before they talk? What difficulties might be looming when children won't play together and should we really make them share?

Such issues hold many 'needing to be researched' questions.

Once the question has been formulated, the action plan begins to flow. It is important to remember that only data that answers the research question should be gathered – other findings, although valuable in themselves, are not part of the research. The research instruments or schedules/charts used to gather and collate the data need to be presented with the findings, so all information should be kept safely as the research proceeds.

Let's look at some concerns voiced by staff considering starting out on the research path.

Q: It can be difficult to know what to record. In the early years, achievements change quickly and sometimes we feel that detailed recordings are overtaken on a daily basis, making them pretty useless.

A: Perhaps when there is no perceived difficulty, i.e. when the child is obviously meeting the different developmental milestones in all aspects of development, too much detail is unnecessary. I think the charts of age-related competencies

---

give a useful first format for recording. These can be set out as a list and boxes can be quickly ticked. Then they can be made more contextually relevant by looking back to the tables describing the learning potential in each area of your particular setting (see Chapter 1). These give more pointers for observation. The main thing is to record objective evidence – it can be cumulative and recorded on a graph to show changing trends if this is appropriate – and that is gleaned from the practitioners' ability to observe on a daily basis.

The question of what these assessments mean is fascinating. To what extent do they form prognoses of what the children will be able to do? What other variables might impinge (social/emotional/genetic influences perhaps)? Why should some children find learning straightforward while others find it perplexingly difficult? These kinds of questions are tackled in earlier chapters and library searches can provide other clues.

This example shows how a starter question can be developed into a really taxing study.

Q: What do you think about using sticky labels for daily recording?

A: That is a splendid way to gather evidence that the children are making progress. The labels should be dated and have the observer's name marked. Different members of staff tend to see particular aspects of development more easily than others – sometimes this is due to their earlier training – and this might bias their recording. So names can be used to check exactly who is saying what. Usually one practitioner stays with the same group of children for some time and this means that a bundle of sticky labels or other notes can be considered together to make a useful cumulative statement for a week or so.

Sometimes a general observation sheet can be prepared to help focus on specific aspects of a problem. Sometimes ideas develop as the process goes on. It is important to record what stimulated further research or caused initial ideas to be changed.

Much more detail is needed if a child has a problem or if a difficulty is suspected. Then shared observations over time are vitally important. This prevents claims that difficulties were 'in the eye of one beholder'. Different kinds of recording charts can be used too. It is important that the child is unaware of being watched and that observations are made on different occasions in a variety of situations.

It is vitally important that observations and assessments of children's difficulties consider each aspect so that any difficulties can be pinpointed and the correct kind of help given. It can be frustrating for a child to be helped to practise the individual movements within a sequence if help is really needed with clarifying the planning, i.e. what movement follows another, or alternatively to be asked about planning when help with the technicalities of the attempted movement is what is required.

Name of Activity . . . .

	Yes	No
1. Can the child do it?	☐	☐

If no,

2. Check   a) Does the child understand the instructions?
              b) Is the level of demand realistic?
              c) Is the equipment suitable?
              d) Are distractions minimised?
              e) Is the child motivated to try?

If a difficulty persists,

3. Identify the movement patterns used.

Please tick			Please tick	
Walking	☐	Climbing	☐
Running	☐	Balancing	☐
Crawling	☐	Twisting	☐
Swinging	☐	Spinning	☐
Turning	☐	Throwing	☐
Stretching	☐	Catching	☐
Jumping	☐	Kicking	☐
Hopping	☐	Aiming	☐
		Being still	

	Yes	No
Study the preparation, action and recovery phases. Is one faulty?	☐	☐

If no,

	Yes	No
4. Is it the transition causing the problem?	☐	☐

What is the main difficulty?		Please tick
	Changing speed	☐
	Changing direction	☐
	Overbalancing	☐
	Fumbling with feet	☐
	Other? If so what	_____

5. Is there a general lack of any underlying movement ability?

	Please tick
Body awareness	☐
Spatial awareness	☐
Rhythmic awareness	☐
Balance	☐
Coordination	☐
Speed of movement	☐

	Yes	No
6. Is the child improving with practice?	☐	☐

Observing children's movement patterns: a chart to aid observation and analysis

from: *Enhancing Learning through Play*, Routledge © 2012 Christine Macintyre

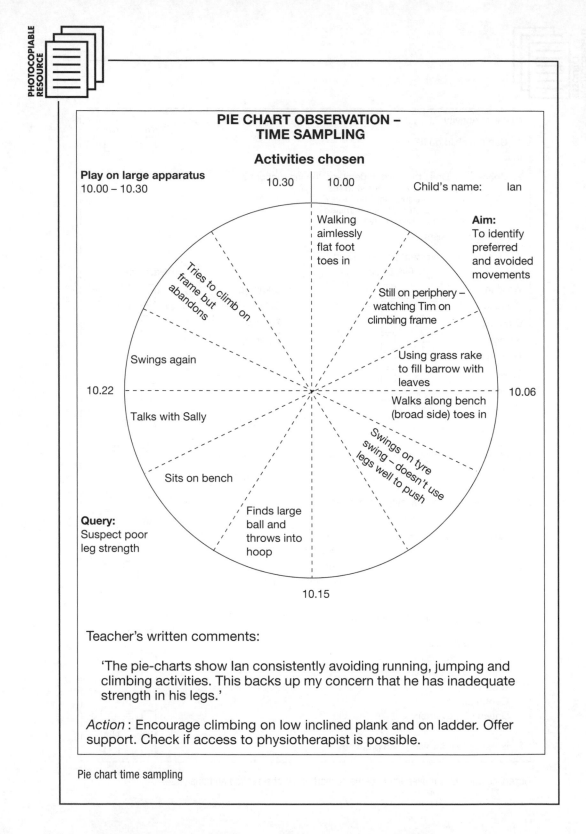

PIE CHART OBSERVATION –
TIME SAMPLING

Activities chosen

Play on large apparatus
10.00 – 10.30

10.30   10.00

Child's name: Ian

Aim:
To identify preferred and avoided movements

Walking aimlessly flat foot toes in

Still on periphery – watching Tim on climbing frame

Tries to climb on frame but abandons

Using grass rake to fill barrow with leaves

Swings again

10.22

10.06

Walks along bench (broad side) toes in

Talks with Sally

Swings on tyre swing – doesn't use legs well to push

Sits on bench

Finds large ball and throws into hoop

Query:
Suspect poor leg strength

10.15

Teacher's written comments:

'The pie-charts show Ian consistently avoiding running, jumping and climbing activities. This backs up my concern that he has inadequate strength in his legs.'

Action : Encourage climbing on low inclined plank and on ladder. Offer support. Check if access to physiotherapist is possible.

Pie chart time sampling

from: *Enhancing Learning through Play*, Routledge © 2012 Christine Macintyre

Q: What would the research be used for?

A: The research findings might be for internal use, to share with others in the setting as an aid to daily or weekly planning, or they might be used to convey information to other professionals such as physiotherapists or speech and language experts if these people are to become partners in supporting specific children. Or the recordings might be part of an extended piece of research where the data contributes to an essay or dissertation. Or a professional in one setting might want to find out what others in different venues thought about a proposed change. Questions might ask about envisaged planning changes and benefits/limitations for the children. There are many ways to develop informal 'chats over the fence' into really scintillating pieces of research that can affect policy-making and enrich children's lives – and yours.

Whatever the issue, there are critical planning issues that should be considered before starting out.

Q: Can you list these rules so that new researchers don't make mistakes?

- The most important preparation is to choose an interesting – to you – area for research – something that intrigues, because the research lasts for some time. The next step is to formulate a research question. This is much more difficult than it sounds. The research question should answer, 'What is it that I want to find out?', and the action plan should take steps to answer that question. Only data to answer that specific question should be collected or the research will become confused.

- The next step is to discuss your plan with others in the setting and/or a tutor, and to trial questions if a questionnaire is to be used. That done, whenever children are involved, get *written* permission from their parents. This is essential. It covers you if parents change their minds or if unforeseen issues arise.

- The parents might be glad of a brief written statement as to why you are carrying out the research. Stress that it is to find a way to support children more effectively.

- Record the steps you are taking to reduce bias in the collection of data and how you will ensure confidentiality.

- Make a time plan and be realistic about what you can do. Set out the plan like a recipe and allocate time to plan, time to record and time to analyse the findings.

- If specific children are to be involved to ascertain whether they have learning differences/difficulties, with experts possibly being called in, then a more formal one-to-one interview with parents needs to be set up.

■ Carefully keep a note of all these early preparations because, especially if the research happens over time, parents can forget they gave permission for their child to be involved and be resentful. Written parental permission is very important, especially if there is to be filming.

Q: Is all of this not a bit OTT?

A: It could seem so, but doing research is a discipline and if 'rules' are not observed then the data may not stand scrutiny. It is easy to knock holes in a piece of research that has not been conceptualised, analysed and reported well. Every step must be clearly documented and every research action must be carefully considered. However it is so good to be able to say that you have discovered something or even have learned to do something new that will benefit the children in your care. Have a go; be prepared for glitches because research is difficult. And above all enjoy it!

(For further information, see C. Macintyre (2000) *The Art of Action Research in the Classroom*, published by David Fulton. In that text, 'the classroom' covers early years and primary years. It was written to support student teachers preparing their final dissertation for a BA (Hons) degree.)

Conclusion:
Bringing It All Together

To me the early years are the most important time in children's lives. During this time we see tremendous changes in all aspects of children's development. They move from being totally dependent to becoming relatively independent and able to make their own way in the setting. They have developed the language to be understood, the emotional strategies to control their feelings; they have learned that others have goals and ambitions and that they must have a turn too. They have become sociocentric rather than egocentric and are anxious to make friends. And when things don't go their own way, they have learned to explain rather than explode! They have the movement abilities to cope with everyday tasks and the skill to run and jump.

But not all children develop in the same ways. Some are anxious to take every learning opportunity while others are reluctant and shy. Some children can't get to play while others are in constant demand. The effects from the children's environment are complex and pervasive. Settings must try to understand the implications of disabilities, even abusive family situations, and compensate for any disadvantages so that the children have the best possible chance to realise their potential. These are not easy things to do.

As children from many different backgrounds come together in nurseries or Families and Children's Centres to sample education (in a more formal sense), they are entering a new world of different demands and complex 'rules'. They need time and space to understand and the security of knowing that they will be able to cope. The staff, too, have a myriad of demands based on decentring, i.e. doing their best to understand each child's participation in the fascinating process that is learning.

We must find the best ways for all our very young children to learn. What are these? Through activity and practical hands-on experience, through enjoyment and challenge, through freedom to develop. These can all be achieved through play for play enhances each child's capacity to learn. Adults are there to support and nurture the children. Surely this is the most important thing for them to do, for it is to the children that the future belongs.

Stepping Stones Showing Progress

The motor milestones

AGE	LOCOMOTOR SKILLS	NON-LOCOMOTOR SKILLS	MANIPULATIVE SKILLS
Birth	Primitive walking reflex and swimming reflex but these will disappear	Will focus at feeding distance: hold eye contact	May hold finger for a moment
4 months	Can sit (briefly) if propped up. Enjoys baby massage and tummy time	Plays with hands as first toy: will hold object briefly; head should be steady, handgrip firm	First attempts at passing objects from hand to hand. Plays with toes – puts toes in mouth
6–9 months	Crawls speedily; some children pulling up to stand; sense of danger evident (two weeks after crawling)	Sitting without support; reaching and grasping more accurately now	Holds toys; feeds self with bottle or finger food. Recognises that dropped objects are still there – seeks to retrieve them
9–12 months	Crawling, walking round furniture, crawling up stairs	Shows preference for some toys; handles them carefully	Scribbles holding pencil firmly. Everything to the mouth for testing texture and taste
12–18 months	Walking securely; will roll over and crawl as a combined action. Rhythmic 'dancing' to music	Does simple puzzles: uses the pincer grip. Enjoys knocking toys over; cares for soft toys – first signs of shared empathy	Will turn the pages of books. Independent feeding. Uses two hands independently
18–24 months	Runs (20 months); walks well (24 months); climbs stairs with both feet on each step	Pushes and pulls boxes or wheeled toys; unscrews lid on a jar	Shows clear hand preference; stacks 4 to 6 blocks; turns pages one at a time; picks

			things up without overbalancing
2–3 years	Runs easily. Climbs up, down and over obstacles unaided	Enjoys drawing and painting with large brush	Picks up small objects (e.g. Cheerios); throws small ball forward while standing
3–4 years	Walks upstairs one foot per step; skips using alternate feet; walks on tiptoe	Pedals and steers a tricycle; walks in any direction pulling a big toy; rotates body when throwing but still little body rotation	Catches large ball between out-stretched arms; cuts paper with scissors; holds pencil between thumb and first two fingers
4–5 years	Walks up and down stairs one foot per step; stands, runs and walks well. Combines actions seamlessly, e.g. run and jump	Boys show mature throwing action; girls enjoy balance challenges such as ballet	Strikes ball with bat; kicks and catches ball; threads beads but not needle; grasps pencil maturely
5–6 years	Skips on alternate feet; walks a thin line; slides, swings	More children show mature turning and kicking action	Plays ball games quite well; threads needle and sews stitches

Development of speech: a developmental plan for speaking

AGE	WORDS	STORIES	ACTIVITIES
5 years	Clear articulation; compound phrases	Can retell a story; suggest new ideas. Can sequence three pictures. Uses pronouns now. May read single words. Likes to have scribing of own ideas done	Can empathise with others' feelings; understands rules and routines. Looks for a friend and will cooperate in a game
4 years	Seeks explanations. Asks 'when?' 'why?' Can visualise events elsewhere	Enjoys repetition and contributing known phrases to stories. Can retell a story or invent one	Can role-play; can understand characterisation. Plays a ball game with a friend
3 years	Uses sentences of 4–5 words; complex use of words	Will listen, adapt and recast sentences. Uses 'why?' constantly. Plays with nonsense words and rhymes	Joins in songs and rhymes. Beats rhythms. Enjoys drawing with coloured chalks
2 years	Huge increase in vocabulary – the naming explosion. Links two words, e.g. 'love you', 'go away'	Follows stories – recognises favourite characters and routines. Gesture and body language combined – holophrases. Communication	Asserts independence – has tantrums. Telegraphic speech, i.e. uses only essential words, e.g. 'I going'

AGE	WORDS	STORIES	ACTIVITIES
		strategies used, e.g. motherese (higher-pitched simplified language)	
1 year	Monosyllabic babbling; 'da, da, da'. Understanding evident from facial expression and gestures	Understands simple instructions, e.g. 'come here'. Can convey wishes through gestures. Understands 50 words: makes own words for wants. Words learned slowly at this pre-linguistic stage	Enjoys peek-a-boo (the basis of turn taking). Memory and a sense of self is developing
3–9 months	Controls gestures; joint attention beginning to develop	Beginning to understand several words. Babbling 'dadadada' on request at 9+ months	Uses smiling to good effect. Claps hands; beginning to point
Birth– 3 months	Cries, increasingly with meaning	Beginning to communicate with gurgles. Cooing	Recognises familiar people as source of comfort

Linking abilities: a developmental framework

AGE	PLAY	LANGUAGE	MOVEMENT
5 years	Can initiate or join in role-play	Can follow a story without pictures. Can read simple words	Can run and jump, ride a bike and zip a coat. Understands the rules of major games
4 years	Understands pretence and develops fears of the unknown. Develops imaginative games, not always able to explain rules	Knows colours and numbers. Can explain events, hopes and disappointments. Able to listen and focus	Can climb and swing on large apparatus. Has a developed sense of safety outdoors. Can swim. Enjoys bunny jumps and balancing activities
3 years	Enjoys group activities, e.g. baking a cake for someone's birthday. Understands turn taking	Uses complex sentences. Understands directional words and simple comparisons, e.g. big/small	Can ride a tricycle and climb stairs. Climbs in and out of cars/buses independently. Can catch a large ball
2½ years	Develops altruism especially for family members. Understands emotional words, e.g. happy, sad	Uses pronouns and past tenses, adding 'ed' to form own version of past tense	Uses a step-together pattern to climb stairs. Can walk some distance

2 years	Beginning to play alongside a friend for a short time (parallel play)	Rebels – says 'no'. Can form two-word sentences but comprehension is far ahead of speech	Can walk well but jumping is still difficult. Climbs on furniture (crawling pattern)
18 months	Sensorimotor play exploring the properties of objects (solitary play)	Has ten naming words. Points to make wishes known	Can crawl at speed and walk but jumping is not developed. Balance is precarious
1 year	Walks unsteadily, arms and step pattern wide to help balance	Enjoys games, e.g. peek-a-boo. Beginning to enjoy books and stories. Monosyllabic babbling	Plays with toys giving them correct usage – simple pretend, e.g. feeding doll
6–8 months	Can sit unsupported briefly. Rolls over. Attempts to crawl	Makes sounds and blows bubbles	Reaching out for objects now. Changing objects from one hand to the other
0–4 months	May be able to support head but weight of head makes this difficult. Strength developing head to toe and centre to periphery. Can lift head briefly when lying on front	Early communication: responds to voices; can make needs known	Plays with hands as first toy. Can hold object placed in hand but cannot let go – object drops

Potential Topics for Study

This list gives ideas that professionals will find helpful in choosing areas for study. From years of helping student teachers find topics for their research projects I found that at the start they found it difficult to decide on a topic, but examples clarified their thinking. There are suggested topics throughout the text – these are other possibilities.

Some ways of honing these down to find research questions are suggested but these have to be contextualised to match the children and the setting. The process is fully explained in my book, *The Art of Action Research in the Classroom* (published by David Fulton). The word 'classroom' is meant to cover any learning experience – home or nursery or school.

1. What are children learning as they play out of doors/in any area? How can I encourage a lone child to become more social?

2. What is the best way to develop a relationship with the parents of a 4-year-old boy who appears to be globally delayed? I have found language strategies that I could share with his parents but they are reluctant to admit there is anything wrong. They say he speaks at home.

3. How can I teach a child to crawl using the cross lateral pattern? What are the implications if she does not crawl?

4. When should children be allowed to take risks? How can we build a safe environment yet one that has the potential for challenges?

5. How do I monitor a child who is extremely bright and does not match any of the tables on developmental norms?

6. Why are two children in the same family so different in their abilities and attitudes?

7. When do children realise that they are either boys or girls. What can I do to avoid gender bias in my setting?

You can take any topic that interests you and then clarify in your mind:

What is it I want to find out?
What action(s) will I take to gather evidence?

How will I record my findings?
What texts, books, papers will provide a starting ground?
How can I assure parents of confidentiality?

Good luck!

Crawling Using the Cross Lateral Pattern

Crawling using the cross lateral pattern is so important because of its links with writing and other fine motor skills, with visual acuity and with crossing the midline. So this appendix gives extra information and some strategies to try to persuade children to adopt this pattern. Over many years talking at conferences and professional development meetings I have asked delegates to get down and crawl! Not everyone liked that, however invariably there were at least two or three who instinctively crawled using the homolateral pattern, i.e. the hand and knee on the same side going forward. And almost always, these bemused adults said they had had difficulties with writing and fine motor skills. Some admitted avoiding all kinds of physical activity. So it is very worthwhile checking how your children crawl and, with game-like activities, urging them to use the cross lateral pattern. Observation can be tricky when the children crawl quickly – if this is the case, ask them to crawl up stairs and this slows the pattern.

There is an age-related sequence of development prior to achieving the crawling action itself (see Table A.1). This helps adults to spot where the children are in developmental terms and when there is a difficulty or a reluctance to try, it gives them an

TABLE A.1 An age-related sequence leading to crawling

20 weeks	Babies can roll over from lying on their backs to their fronts (supine to prone lying). They rotate their upper body then twist a leg over. This is a natural preparation for crawling
28 weeks	Babies can roll over and push up supporting the weight of the upper body by the arms. The trunk is still low
32 weeks	Movement forward begins but this is usually a pulling forward on the arms action with the trunk still low
36 weeks	Gradually a raised crawling position is achieved – often a rocking action – hands and feet with bottom in the air is practised and this is important in eliminating the asymmetric tonic neck reflex
44 weeks	Progress – locomotion on hands and knees happens

indication of what preliminary stages could be helpful. Four-year-olds can show you if they can roll over – they don't need to know it is a 'test'!

NB Unless there is a difficulty, children will go through this sequence of events when they are ready, when they have the strength and the neurological maturation to allow this to happen. It is an innate progression, down to nature rather than nurture. Some children will be skilled crawlers at 7 months, others will wait until they are 17 months, and both are fine. And many will take themselves through this sequence with no prompting or teaching needed. But if there is delay or a reluctance to adopt the cross lateral pattern, then knowing the sequence can prevent adults stressing the children by asking them to progress too quickly.

Q: What can I do to ensure my child is strong enough to crawl?

A: From the early weeks give your child plenty of tummy time. This encourages pushing up to see and strengthens the neck, arm and shoulder muscles. You will gradually see the child attempt to pull along the floor and you can be reassured that progress is being made. Reluctant-to-move children may be encouraged by asking them to stretch one arm out for a toy, but adults should not harry the children unnecessarily. They will make progress when they have the strength and the neurological competence to do so. Children have an inbuilt motivation to move. Sometimes adults must just wait. Allied to that, of course, is the number of opportunities babies are given. If they sit in a buggy all day, then practice sessions are missed. Once professionals in settings understand the implications of this, I hope they will share them with the parents and/or carers and that they in turn will give the children many opportunities to crawl.

Q: What else can we look out for?

A: With your child in the table position, stand in front and dangle a toy so that the head is raised. Check that the child can retain the table position and does not flop back. Attaining and holding the table position shows that the child's vestibular sense or sense of balance is working well. Balance is very important. It is 'vital for posture, movement and it contributes to a developing sense of self' (Bee and Boyd 2005) and so affects the self-esteem. And as all other sensory input passes through the balance mechanism en route to analysis in the higher centres of the brain, an underdeveloped vestibular sense can hinder all aspects of learning (see Chapter 3).

Q: If children avoid crawling, if being put on their front distresses them, what does it mean?

A: Some babies and toddlers don't immediately take to this but gentle encouragement – perhaps another child alongside, or even mum – can help them. Just keep the activity short and gradually increase the time as the child gains confidence. It is really worthwhile persevering.

Q: Is there anything else we can do to help?

A: (1) With the child in a table position, play a game 'rocking from toes to hands' as children at the earlier stage of learning to crawl do. This action can help to inhibit a retained asymmetric tonic neck reflex. (2) Take crawling back through the stages in the table. Learning to crawl using the cross lateral pattern gives the brain a second chance to make connections and achieve the most useful pathways.

Q: This is amazing. Are there any other benefits?

A: Crawling also promotes social and emotional gains. The social gains come when the child crawls to meet or join in a game with another person, and the emotional gains come from the achievement that probably merits praise, and the 'feeling of being-able-to-do' that enhances self-confidence and self-esteem.

Q: When the children can crawl should we do anything more?

A: It's a good idea to have crawling activities every day. This can be crawling up stairs, in and out of table legs or on a climbing frame. In this next picture, although Gareth has actually achieved the cross lateral pattern, when he tries to crawl through the hoops his feet fall out to the side. Now most children would immediately retract them but Gareth doesn't because he doesn't really feel where his feet are. So he has to wait and think and look back at his feet then pull them in. All of this takes time and extra concentration.

An action that should be automatic has to be done at the much slower conscious level. So careful observation of crawling can also reveal poor body awareness.

Q: What can be done to help this?

A: For the younger ones extend the ideas in the favourite rhyme 'Heads, shoulders, knees and toes' to bring in other body parts. The rhyme below shows how.

> Heads, shoulders, knees and toes, knees and toes,
> Heads, shoulders, knees and toes, knees and toes,
> Eyes and ears and chin and nose,
> Heads, shoulders, knees and toes.
>
> Heads, shoulders, knees and toes, knees and toes,
> Heels, bottoms, backs and nose, backs and nose,
> Tap your shoulders, turn right round,
> Stretch to the sky – don't make a sound.
>
> Make your fingers stretch out wide, stretch out wide.
> Now clap your hands against your side, against your side.
> Make them whirl you round and round, then
> Sit very quietly on the ground, on the ground.

In this extended version of the rhyme, in verse 2, the tapping comes up the back rather than going down the front. This makes children aware of these parts of their bodies. Few activities ask children to be aware of their backs and as they can't see their backs this body part gets ignored. Can you think of any activities or songs that you use that refer to backs?

Then the 'tap your shoulders' line asks the children to cross their hands in front to tap their opposite shoulder. This, apart from promoting shoulder awareness, shows observers whether they can cross the midline of the body. Some children find this very difficult – it is as if there is a wall there. This could be part of a retained reflex and should be noted and expert help requested if the difficulty persists. If you are in doubt, ask the children to paint wide rainbows in the sky and see if they change hands at the apex of the arc. This idea of crossing can be expanded to use the knees (in front and behind), the elbows and the ankles, and once these games have been played and the children have learned all about the different body parts, the 'Simon says' game make a natural and useful progression.

In verse 3, stretching to the side develops spatial awareness and this contrasts with the hand and arm actions that 'clap against the side'. Stretching out and holding that position can be a difficult balance challenge so it's best to keep the rhythm brisk. The clapping against the sides provides a fun release and helps develop body awareness of where the sides are in relation to other body parts.

So in a simple game we have introduced the heels, the shoulders, the back and the sides, the elbows and the ankles and the back of the knees. That's good because we don't talk much about these parts, do we?

My recommendation would be that jingles and crawling practice happened every single day. (For ideas about linking jingles with stories and poems see C. Macintyre, *Jingle Time* (2002).) Challenges can be introduced by having children crawling over and under and through obstacles, round table legs and up stairs. This keeps the play challenging and fun.

2. If your partner uses the cross lateral pattern effortlessly, i.e. one hand and the opposite knee forward, change over and you try.

3. If your partner instinctively crawls using the homolateral pattern, suggest he/she changes and watch to see how difficult adopting the cross lateral pattern is.

4. If the homolateral pattern is the natural one, ask about any writing difficulties, for this is a key link. Ask about the birth; was it a C-section or a breech birth? Was bum shuffling the preferred method of getting around?

5. In the crawling position, ask your partner to stretch out one leg or arm – or both at the same time. Is balancing an issue?

6. Above all, check that the children in your setting can crawl using the cross lateral pattern. Especially if they have difficulties, play crawling games every day, no matter how old the children are. It is never too late to help!

A Record for Assessment

This record is for two colleagues to share in gathering preliminary evidence about a child's difficulties. Each section asks each teacher to independently give a mark out of 10. This does four things:

1. It allows teachers to recognise that two professionals can see different things.
2. It focuses assessments on specifics rather than global estimations.
3. It highlights the interplay of recordings to try to find causes of difficulties.
4. It gives the teacher confidence in taking assessments on to the next stage and explaining this to the parents – which is not always what parents want to hear.

Confidentiality: it goes without saying that records and assessments have to be kept confidential within the school even after parents' permission has been granted. Knowing this, parents will be more likely to let their child participate in support groups. You would of course explain that the child would not be singled out but would participate in small groups, or whatever your plan was.

Once parents have been reassured, confidentiality has to be respected at every turn. Only in this way can sound relationships and shared strategies between home and school be developed.

The checklist now asks you to tick one box for each competence then give a mark out of 10 for 'general coping ability' in that field. The alternatives are: 'Yes, can do it'; 'Some difficulty', meaning that the child needs real effort to cope; 'Severe difficulty', meaning that the child does not cope; and 'Regression', which means that the child's performance is getting worse.

Please give further information at any point if you feel this would be appropriate. This could concern the areas already mentioned or different topics.

Thank you for completing this!

A Movement Observation Record

Child's name .... Sex ❏ Male ❏ Female

Age............... years .... months

This checklist is for a child who is causing you concern. Please record the child's usual level of competence rather than focusing on one unusual occurrence. If, however, the child's movement is erratic, making a general picture difficult or less than useful, please say that this is the case.

Before looking more specifically at motor development, please note whether you would consider that this was the child's only area of difficulty or whether there are other problems too. NB This is a movement observation record to help teachers compile assessment profiles for school use or for gaining access to specialist help. It is not a test to diagnose dyspraxia.

Please tick if appropriate and add any other areas of concern.

	Yes	No
Does the child have:		
(a) Poor sight	❏	❏
(b) Low hearing	❏	❏
(c) A physical disability	❏	❏
(d) Difficulty in understanding instructions	❏	❏
(e) Speech difficulties	❏	❏
(f) Body-build problems:	❏	❏
(i) Overweight enough to hamper movement	❏	❏
(ii) A fragile build that makes the child wary	❏	❏
(iii) Poor muscle tone: little strength	❏	❏
And is the child:		
(g) Very tense and unsure	❏	❏
(h) Aggressive	❏	❏
(i) Lethargic – hard to interest	❏	❏
(j) Lacking persistence	❏	❏
(k) Seeking attention all the time	❏	❏

Any other difficulty? Please note below.

Gross Motor Skills

Can the child:	Yes, can do it	Some difficulty	Severe difficulty	Regression	Please give details
(a) Stand still, balanced and in control?					
(b) Sit at a desk or table without slumping?					
(c) Sit still retaining poise?					
(d) Crawl using the cross lateral pattern?					
(e) Walk smoothly and with good poise?					
(f) Turn corners efficiently?					

from: *Enhancing Learning through Play*, Routledge © 2012 Christine Macintyre

	Yes, can do it	Some difficulty	Severe difficulty	Regression	Please give details
(g) Walk (tandem, heel toe) for 2 metres? Note arm curling forward					
(h) Jump (two feet off floor)?					
(i) Kick a stationary ball in the correct direction? Note tracking					
(j) Catch a large soft ball when thrown sympathetically?					
(k) Roll (pencil roll) and recover to stand with a good sense of timing and balance?					
Give a mark out of 10 for coordination in gross motor skills					
Please give further details if appropriate					

from: *Enhancing Learning through Play*, Routledge © 2012 Christine Macintyre

Fine Motor Skills

	Yes, can do it	Some difficulty	Severe difficulty	Regression	Please give details
Can the child:					
(a) Use a pencil/paintbrush with control?					
(b) Pick up and replace objects efficiently?					
(c) Use two hands together to thread beads, build Lego or do jigsaws?					
(d) Cross the midline with either hand?					
(e) Draw a circle? Draw a person with some detail of parts?					
(f) Dress in the correct order?					
Give a mark out of 10 for dexterity in fine motor skills					
Please give further details if appropriate					

from: *Enhancing Learning through Play*, Routledge © 2012 Christine Macintyre

Intellectual Skills

Can the child:	Yes, can do it	Some difficulty	Severe difficulty	Regression	Please give details
(a) Talk readily to adults? Talk readily to children?					
(b) Articulate clearly?					
(c) Use a wide vocabulary?					
(d) Listen attentively?					
(e) Respond appropriately?					
(f) Follow a sequence of instructions?					
(g) Understand:					
(i) spatial concepts – over, under, through?					
(ii) simple mathematical concepts – bigger, smaller?					

Give the child a mark out of 10 for intellectual competence

Please give further details if appropriate

from: *Enhancing Learning through Play*, Routledge © 2012 Christine Macintyre

Social Skills

Can the child:	Yes, can do it	Some difficulty	Severe difficulty	Regression	Please give details
(a) Take turns with no fuss?					
(b) Interact easily with other children?					
(c) Take the lead in activities?					
(d) Participate in someone else's game?					
Give the child a mark out of 10 for social behaviour					

from: *Enhancing Learning through Play*, Routledge © 2012 Christine

Emotional Skills

Does the child:	Usually	Sometimes	Rarely	Regression	Please give details
(a) Appear confident in following the daily routine?					
(b) Constantly seek attention?					
(c) Disturb other children?					
(d) Sustain eye contact?					
(e) Cope in new situations?					
(f) Appear aggressive or defiant?					
Give the child a mark out of 10 for emotional behaviour					

from: *Enhancing Learning through Play*, Routledge © 2012 Christine Macintyre

Bibliography

Aaron, J. (2006) 'NFAT dysregulation by increased dosage of DSCR11 and DYRKIA on chromosome 21', *Nature* 441: 595–9.

Ainsworth, M.D.S. (1972) 'Attachment and dependency: a comparison', in J.L. Gewirtz (ed.) *Attachment and Dependency*. Washington, DC: V.H. Winston.

Bandura, A. (1992) 'Social cognitive theory', in R. Vasta (ed.) *Six Theories of Child Development*. London: Jessica Kingsley.

Barnardos (2002) *Believe in Children*. London: Barnardos.

Baumrind, D. (1991) 'Current patterns of parental authority', *Developmental Psychology Monographs* 4 (1, part 2).

Bee, H. and Boyd, D. (2005) *The Developing Child*, international edn. Boston: Pearson.

Best Practice Network (n.d.) *Standards for Early Years Professional Status*. Bristol: Best Practice Network.

Bigler, R.S. (2000) 'The role of classification skill in moderating environmental influences on children's gender stereotyping: a study of functional use of gender in the classroom', *Child Development* 66: 1072–87.

Bowlby, J. (1988) *A Secure Base*. New York: Basic Books.

Bruner, J.S. (1966) *The Process of Education*. Cambridge, MA: Harvard University Press.

Bryson, M. (2000) 'The development of Language', unpublished PhD thesis, University of Edinburgh.

Buss, A.H. and Plomin, R. (1986) 'The EAS approach to temperament', in R. Plomin and J. Dunn (eds) *The Study of Temperament, Changes, Continuities and Challenges*. Hillsdale, NJ: Erlbaum, pp. 67–80.

Cacioppo, J.T. and Patrick, W. (2008) *Loneliness*. New York: Norton.

Carter, R. (2000) *Mapping the Mind*. London: Phoenix Books.

City of Edinburgh Council (2008) *A Curriculum for Excellence*. Edinburgh: City of Edinburgh Council.

Claxton, D. (1997) *Hare Brain, Tortoise Mind*. London: Fourth Estate.

Claxton, G. (1990) *Teaching to Learn: A Direction for Education*. London: Cassell.

Cohen, D. (1987) *The Development of Play*. New York: University Press.

Collins, M. (2005) *It's OK to Be Sad*. Bristol: Lucky Duck Publishing.

Cooper, H. (ed.) (2004) *Exploring Time and Place Through Play*. London: David Fulton.

Corlett, L. (2006) *Attention Deficit Hyperactivity Disorder: A Guide to Intervention and Management of Pupils with ADHD*. Edinburgh: Edinburgh City Psychological Services.

Crittenden, P.M. (2008) *Raising Parents: Attachment, Parenting and Child Safety*. Cullompton: Willan Publishing.

DfES (Department for Education and Skills) (2004) *Every Child Matters: Change for Children*. London: DfES.

DfES (Department for Education and Skills) (2007) *Statutory Framework for the Early Years Foundation Stage: Setting the Standards for Learning, Development and Care of Children from Birth to Five*. Nottingham: DfES.

Dixon, P. (2005) *Let Me Be: A Cry for the Rights of Creativity and Childhood in Education*. Winchester: Peche Luna Press.

Dowling, M. (2004) *Young Children's Personal, Social and Emotional Development*. London: Paul Chapman Publishing.

Draper, I.T. (1993) *Lecture Notes on Neurology*. Oxford: Blackwell Scientific Publications.

Dunn, J. and Kendrick, C. (1982) *Sibling Love, Envy and Understanding*. Cambridge, MA: Harvard University Press.

Eron, L.D., Huesmann, L.R. and Zelli, A. (1991) 'The role of parental variables in the learning of aggression', in D.I. Pepler and K.H. Rubin (eds) *The Development and Treatment of Childhood Aggression*. Hillsdale, NJ: Erlbaum, pp. 169–88.

Freeman, J. (2010) *Gifted Lives: What Happens When Gifted Children Grow Up?* London: Routledge.

Gardner, H. (1983) *Frames of Mind: The Theory of Multiple Intelligences*. New York: Basic Books.

Gardner, H. (2007) *Five Minds for the Future*. Cambridge, MA: Harvard University Press.

Goddard, S. (1996) *A Teacher's Window into the Child's Mind*. Eugene, OR: Fern Ridge Press.

Goddard Blythe, S. (2005) *The Well-Balanced Child*. Stroud: Hawthorn Press, Early Years Series.

Goddard Blythe, S. (2008) *What Babies and Children Really Need*. Stroud: Hawthorn Press, Early Years Series.

Goodenough, F.L. (1972) *Anger in Young Children*. Minneapolis, MN: University of Minnesota Press.

Harris, P. (1992) *Children and Emotion: The Development of Psychological Understanding*. Oxford: Blackwell.

Hartup, W.W. (1992) 'Peer relations in early and middle childhood', in V.B. Van Hasselt and N. Hersen (eds) *Handbook of Social Development: A Lifespan Perspective*. New York: Plenum Press.

Honing, H., Ladinig, O., Haden, G.P. and Winkler, I. (2009) 'Is beat induction innate or learned? The neurosciences and music III – disorders and plasticity', *Annals of the New York Academy of Sciences* 1169: 93–6.

Hughes, A. (2010) *Developing Play for the Under-3s*. London: David Fulton Publishers.

Hutt, C. (1979) *Play as Learning, Play as Practice in Teaching Children 0–5*. Oxford: Blackwell.

Isaacs, S. (1933) *Social Development in Young Children*. London: Routledge & Kegan Paul.

Kuczaj, S.A. (1981) 'Factors affecting children's hypothetical reference', *Journal of Child Language* 8: 131–7.

Kurdek, L.A. and Fine, M.A. (1994) 'Family acceptance and family control as predictors of adjustment in young adolescents', *Child Development* 65: 1137–46.

Lee, K. (2010) *Little Liars Grow up to Be Great Leaders*. Research Report: Institute of Child Study. Toronto: Toronto University Press.

Lewis, C., Freeman, N.H., Kyriakidou, C., Maridaki-Kassotaki, K. and Berridge, D.M. (1996) 'Social Influences on false belief access: specific sibling influences?' *Child Development* 67: 2930–47.

Lewis, T.L., Amini, F. and Lannon, R. (2000) *A General Theory of Love*. New York: Vintage.

Locke, A. (2008) 'A summary of the development of language and communication from birth to six years', paper presented at the Early Years Conference, Durham.

Macintyre, C. (2001) *Enhancing Learning Through Play*. London: David Fulton Publishers.

Macintyre, C. (2002a) *Early Intervention in Movement*. London: David Fulton Publishers.

Macintyre, C. (2002b) *The Art of Action Research in the Classroom*. London: David Fulton Publishers.

Macintyre, C. (2003) *Jingle Time: Rhymes and Songs for Early Years Settings*. London: Routledge.

Macintyre, C. (2007) *Understanding Children's Development in the Early Years*. London: David Fulton Publishers.

Macintyre, C. (2009a) *Dyspraxia in the Early Years*, 2nd edn. London: David Fulton Publishers.

Macintyre, C. (2009b) *Bullying and Young Children*. London: David Fulton Publishers.

Macintyre, C. (2010) *Play for Children with Special Needs*, 2nd edn. London: David Fulton Publishers.

Macintyre, C. (2011) *Understanding Babies and Young Children from Conception to Three: A Guide for Students, Practitioners and Parents*. London: Routledge.

Meadows, S. and Cashdan, A. (1998) *Helping Children Learn: Contributions to a Cognitive Curriculum*. London: David Fulton Publishers.

Moore, K.L. and Persaud, T.V.N. (1993) *The Developing Human: Clinically Oriented Embryology*, 5th edn. Philadelphia, PA: Saunders.

Murdoch, E. and Macintyre C. (2005) 'Assessing in the affective domain', Edinburgh: Dunfermline College of Physical Education.

Neihart, M. (2003) 'Gifted children with ADHD', ERIC EC Digest 649, *Journal of the Support for Learning Association* (ILSA), Dublin.

Paley, V.G. (2004) *A Child's Work: The Importance of Fantasy Play*. Chicago, IL: University of Chicago Press.

Palmer, S. (2006) *Toxic Childhood*. London: Orion Books.

Palmer, S. (2009) *21st Century Boys*. London: Orion Books.

Peer, L. (2002) 'Otitis media: a new hypothesis in dyslexia', paper presented at the BDA International Conference, University of Warwick.

Pettit, G.S., Clawson, M.A., Dodge, K.A. and Bates, J.E. (2006) 'Stability and change in peer rejected status: the role of child behaviour, parenting and family ecology', *Merrill-Palmer Quarterly* 42: 295–318.

Piaget, J. (1951) *Play, Dreams and Imitation in Childhood*. London: Routledge Classics.

Piaget, J. (1969) *The Psychology of the Child*. New York: Basic Books.

Piaget, J. (1977) *The Development of Thought: Equilibration of Cognitive Structures*. New York: Viking Press.

Piaget, J. and Inhelder, B. (1969) *The Psychology of the Child*. New York: Basic Books.

Portwood, M. (1998) *Developmental Dyspraxia: Identification and Intervention: A Manual for Parents and Professionals*, 2nd edn. London: David Fulton Publishers.

Robinson, M. (2011) *Understanding Behaviour and Development in Early Childhood: A Guide to Theory and Practice*. London: Routledge.

Rubin, K.H., Hymel, S., Mills, R.S.L. and Rose-Krasnor, L. (1983) 'Play', in E.M. Hetherington (ed.) *Handbook of Child Psychology: Socialization, Personality and Social Development*, Vol. 4. New York: Wiley.

Sternberg, R.J. (1985) *Beyond IQ: A Triarchic Theory of Human Intelligence*. New York: Cambridge University Press.

Stunkard, A.J. and Sobel, J. (1995) *Psychosocial Consequences of Obesity*. New York: Guilford Press.

Sunderland, M. (2006a) *The Science of Parenting*. London: Dorling Kindersley.

Sutherland, M. (2006b) 'The key relational needs of the child', paper presented at the Sunderland Conference on Child Development, Bolden.

Taylor, M. (1993) 'A developmental investigation of children's imaginary companions', *Developmental Psychology* 29: 276–85.

Thomas, A. and Chess, S. (1977) *Temperament and Development*. New York: Brunner/Mazel.

Trevarthen, C. (1977) *Play for Tomorrow*. Edinburgh University Video Production.

Vygotsky, L.S. (1978) *Mind and Society*. Cambridge, MA: Harvard University Press.

Winkley, D. (2004) 'Grey matters: current neurological research and its implications for educators', seminar: www.keele.ac.uk/depts/ed/kisnet/interviews/winkley.htm

Winston, R. (2004) *The Human Mind and How to Make the Most of it*. London: Bantam Books.

Index